THE POWER OF WORDS

THE POWER OF WORDS

Developing a Vocabulary Rich Culture in Reception

Emma Cate Stokes

CORWIN

1 Oliver's Yard
55 City Road
London EC1Y 1SP

CORWIN
A Sage company
2455 Teller Road
Thousand Oaks, California 91320
(800)233-9936
www.corwin.com

Unit No 323-333, Third Floor, F-Block
International Trade Tower, Nehru Place
New Delhi 110 019

8 Marina View Suite 43-053
Asia Square Tower 1
Singapore 018960

Editor: Delayna Spencer
Editorial assistant: Harry Dixon
Production editor: Rabia Barkatulla
Copyeditor: Diana Chambers
Indexer: Silvia Benvenuto
Marketing manager: Dilhara Attygalle
Cover design: Wendy Scott
Typeset by: KnowledgeWorks Global Ltd
Printed and bound in Great Britain by
CPI Group (UK) Ltd, Croydon, CR0 4YY

© 2025 Emma Stokes

Apart from any fair dealing for the purposes of research, private study, or criticism or review, as permitted under the Copyright, Designs and Patents Act, 1988, this publication may not be reproduced, stored or transmitted in any form, or by any means, without the prior permission in writing of the publisher, or in the case of reprographic reproduction, in accordance with the terms of licences issued by the Copyright Licensing Agency. Enquiries concerning reproduction outside those terms should be sent to the publisher.

Library of Congress Control Number: 2024934806

British Library Cataloguing in Publication data

A catalogue record for this book is available from the British Library

ISBN 9781529779516
ISBN 9781529779509 (pbk)

For Dad.
Without you, none of this would be possible.

CONTENTS

About the Author ix
Acknowledgements xi

1 Introduction: How do Words Work? 1

2 Does the EYFS Framework and 'Development Matters' Guide Effective Vocabulary Teaching in Reception? 15

3 How do Children Learn? 33

4 Which Words? 47

5 The GUIDE Framework: How do I Plan a Lesson? 63

6 How do I Teach Concept Words? 81

7 Talk, Talk, Talk: How Can I Make Every Word Count? 99

8 How do I Make Play Purposeful? 117

9 How Can I Empower Every Child's Vocabulary Journey? 131

10 What are My Next Steps? 149

References 151
Index 155

ABOUT THE AUTHOR

Emma Cate is a former teacher and Early Years and Key Stage 1 leader. In her spare time, she writes about pedagogy at emmacateteaching.com. She co-founded #PrimaryEssentials, an annual online conference providing CPD for primary teachers. As an educational writer, she has contributed to *TES*, *Schools Week*, *The Headteacher*, *Teachwire* and *Teach Primary*. She is also the editor of edtechinnovationhub.com, where she curates the latest EdTech news and views. Her personal interests include being a proud cat lady, a book and film geek and a tech nerd. She can often be found under a blanket, a cat in her lap and a book in her hand. You can find her on X (formerly Twitter): @emmccatt and LinkedIn on: www.linkedin.com/in/emmcatestokes/

ACKNOWLEDGEMENTS

First and foremost, I want to thank my incredible fiancé and best friend, Scott. Thank you for being my biggest cheerleader. Your belief in me lifts me up. I love you.

Thank you to my fur baby Oliver, who has been there for a cuddle whenever I have had writer's block.

I am forever grateful to my mum, who has encouraged my love of reading from a young age and from whom I inherited my bossy teacher traits – which, let's face it, has been both a blessing and a curse!

Thank you to my dad, whom I miss every single day. Your encouragement and support started me off on this wild teaching journey. I hope you're up there, smiling down at the teacher I've become.

I'm beyond grateful for my amazing family. Thank you to Nanny Kit, Nanny Pam, Grandpa Stu, Laura, Francis, Annet, and my niece and nephew, the loves of my life.

This book journey has been a rollercoaster. It started in the midst of COVID-19 and paused for a significant amount of time while I battled some health issues. The constant support of my best friends got me through. Thank you, Ellie, Ros, Kate and my peas – Amy and Shannen.

A heartfelt thank you to my Twitter family. Being sick and isolated, you all made me feel less alone. Sophie, Nimi, Dee, Ben, Luke, Sarah, Mia, Stuart – you are all amazing humans.

I have endless gratitude to my editor, Delayna, Harry and the whole Sage team. You've been patient, supportive and just plain amazing.

I wouldn't be here today without the wonderful teachers and school staff I have had the pleasure of working with and learning from. Teaching is the best profession in the world, and I can't imagine being me without it. I am privileged to have been mentored by some incredible educators. Thank you, Marian, Jo and Katie.

Thank you, Kate, Katy and Louise for being the best colleagues anyone could ever ask to work with. You made the toughest days bearable and the good days wonderful.

Finally, thank you to the person reading this. Thank you for being part of our profession. Thank you for shaping little hearts and minds and helping them develop. Ironically, words cannot express how grateful I am to you for reading this book. Thank you from the bottom of my heart.

1

INTRODUCTION: HOW DO WORDS WORK?

Words are powerful. Individual words hold their own unique meanings. When organised into appropriate grammatical structures, words are used to communicate. They are the primary way that the majority of human beings interact with each other within society to share common ideas. A robust and wide-reaching vocabulary enhances all forms of interaction, be it speaking, listening, reading or writing. Word understanding enables us to fully connect to the lyrics of a song or feel tears spring to our eyes when we read poignant prose. They can define a person via their expression of ideas, debate, emotion and opinion. The power of words cannot be underestimated or overvalued. They are essential to being human and arguably humanity's greatest achievement.

This book examines the complexities of vocabulary acquisition in Reception class by concisely summarising language-based research and how this can be transitioned into the classroom.

Teachers, by the very nature of the job, are incredibly busy. Time is a valuable commodity. As a former practising teacher, I am well aware of time constraints and workload that can mean practitioners have limited time to read and dissect complex research.

The Power of Words: Developing a Vocabulary Rich Culture in Reception takes complex key theories and research alongside case studies and brings them together in an accessible way for Reception teachers and those interested in vocabulary acquisition to implement in the classroom.

WHY DO WORDS MATTER?

It is common knowledge that early language experiences play a crucial part in the development of young children. With Communication and Language forming one of the three prime areas within the EYFS, we know how integral words are for a child's development. Words form the foundations of our teaching and of a child's learning. A study by Fernald et al. in 2013 revealed that by 18 months, toddlers from different socioeconomic groups show dramatic differences in their vocabularies. By 24 months, this disparity grows significantly, with children from higher economic backgrounds processing language more quickly and accurately than their peers from lower economic groups. For some children, there is already a huge vocabulary deficit even before entering school.

Often quoted, the Hart and Risley study from 1995 and updated in 2003 shared their widely disseminated research in the nineties, which collected data from 42 families that covered a range of socioeconomic statuses. For two and a half years, they recorded children aged 7 months to 3 years monthly to observe their language environment. Their findings showed that within the families observed, children in the upper-income homes were spoken to more regularly than their lower-income counterparts, seemingly leading to a 30-million word gap.

More recently, newer evidence that has come to light has shown this is not as black and white as it first appears. A seeming replication of the original study from Sperry et al. (2019) suggests that while there are vast differences in young children's language environments, these differences are spread equally across socioeconomic backgrounds. Essentially, children are exposed to varying words, but this exposure to less cannot be consigned to a particular socioeconomic background.

Now, while this study was a replica in terms of the number of families involved, the socioeconomic backgrounds of the families were not *exactly* the same. In Hart and Risley's original study (1995), the largest language gap was between the higher-income socioeconomic children and those whose caregivers received welfare from the state. However, the Sperry et al. (2019) study did not have that higher-income sample. It can be argued that there was insufficient economic diversity within the study.

With 4.2 million children living in poverty in the UK (Child Poverty Action Group, 2023) – that's an average of 9 children in a class of 30 – this is something that all teachers should be reflecting upon, regardless. Teaching predominantly in schools with pupils from disadvantaged backgrounds – and coming from one myself – I have always believed that these children should get the best possible education. For many, an excellent education is their one shot. They don't have the same privileges as middle-class children to fall back on if it doesn't work out the first time around.

All that being said, what is integral from both studies is that young children have a vast range of language experiences before they even enter our Reception classrooms. We know that the understanding of vocabulary can have considerable effects in other areas of learning (Cunningham and Stanovich, 1997). Children with extensive vocabulary knowledge are far more likely to use a broader range of words in their language, allowing for greater development of abstract thinking than peers with limited vocabulary.

Limited vocabulary knowledge can also lead to limited comprehension both in day-to-day interaction in the provision, during storytime and when the child starts to read independently.

All this paints a bleak picture, but Reception teachers are in the ideal position to combat this. For many of our young learners, the Reception year is where the primary journey begins. It is where the foundations are laid. For this reason (among others), I would argue that it is the most important year in primary school. Montag et al.'s (2018) research has shown that both the quality and quantity of early language experience and exposure will have a marked effect on a child's development, especially in how they engage with learning in an educational setting.

When children enter the Reception classroom, they are introduced daily to multitudes of brand-new words. Teaching children the fundamentals of language is one of the most important aspects of the Early Years. With that in mind, Reception teachers must make every moment of vocabulary teaching count. I don't believe in wasting time on things that will not further their learning and development. Every minute those children are with me is a minute I cannot give back to them, so every minute has to matter.

KEY TAKEAWAYS

- Early language is integral to the development of children.
- Studies suggest that poverty widens the early word gap.
- As Reception is the beginning of many children's learning journey, Reception teachers are in the ideal position to counteract the vocabulary deficit.

Pause for Reflection

Reflect on how you address the diverse language backgrounds and potential vocabulary deficits in your Reception cohort, considering the varied language exposures across socioeconomic backgrounds. How do you ensure that your vocabulary teaching is impactful and tailored to meet each child's needs, recognising the crucial role of the Reception year in setting the foundation for their linguistic and educational journey?

FULLY KNOWING A WORD

A word is the smallest unit of language that works independently. Words are seen as independent when they can be separated from other words and move within a sentence.

To be independent, a word:

- must not depend on other words and can be separated from other units;
- can change position within a sentence.

The simplest way of describing words is that they convey meaning. Linguist Ray Jackendoff says, 'What makes a word a word is that it is a pairing between a pronounceable piece of sound and a meaning' (Jackendoff, 2012: 124). But what gives words meaning?

To teach words effectively, it is essential to know what it means to fully understand a word. We know that words are a form of communication via language. Language is our ability to produce and comprehend both spoken and written words. Ironically, some words below may not immediately provoke meaning for you. They didn't for me when I first encountered them, but meaning is produced when words are explained and broken down.

Grammar

Often described as a set of rules, I prefer to think of grammar as a language system. If we think of grammar as a set of rules, we are insinuating that the rules were consciously created before language. We know this is not the case. Languages evolve. They start with sounds, which in turn become words, which in turn become sentences. Grammar helps us navigate this. It is how words, phrases and clauses work together to create meaning within language.

Phonemes

Phonemes form part of phonics and are something we work on from day one with our students due to their integral role in early reading.

A phoneme is the smallest unit in a given language and holds its own distinct meaning. A phoneme can often be the singular thing that differentiates one word from another. The 'b' in 'bat' holds a different meaning from the 'c' in 'cab'. There are 44 phonemes in the English language that can be put together to make words.

Graphemes

Similar to phonemes, graphemes are something that Reception teachers should know intimately as they also form part of phonics teaching. When specifically discussing the English language, a grapheme is a way of writing a phoneme. They are commonly made up of one, two, three or four letters.

In other languages, a grapheme is the smallest unit of a written language and can include a variety of printed symbols, such as punctuation marks. It does not necessarily correspond to a single phoneme, but may also represent syllables or units of meaning. As this book will be focusing on the English language, it will refer to graphemes in the English language context.

Morphemes

This a small segment of language that is either a word or part of a word. They can be seen as *free morphemes* in that they function as words on their own – e.g., eat, kick, smile. They can also be *bound morphemes* which cannot function as words and must be combined with another morpheme to create a word. In English, bound morphemes are normally affixes (prefixes or suffixes) – e.g., eats, kicks, smiles, unhappy.

Understanding how words and word parts correlate is key to comprehensive understanding. The word 'dog' is closely related to 'dogs' as it is plural. To understand the relationship, we must first understand plurals and their functions.

Word Classes

Sentences have structures that are generally followed so they make sense to those communicating. In English, words fall into eight main word classes according to their role within sentences: nouns, determiners, pronouns, verbs, adjectives, adverbs, prepositions and conjunctions. Every word belongs to one of these categories.

Syntax

When choosing the words we wish to express, we have to arrange those words to make sense. Our syntax is how we put word categories and morphemes in an order that allows us to communicate effectively in phrases and sentences.

Semantics

Often used in the phrase 'That's just semantics' to dismiss an argument as lacking in substance, semantics is actually a language understanding heavyweight. Simply put, semantics is how we interpret words, signs, sentence structure and the meaning conveyed to us. Semantics can determine our understanding of others and has a large part to play in reading comprehension.

Register

Our register is the way a speaker navigates language in different circumstances. We use our register in various communications, such as writing, speaking and signing. When speaking, it is the words chosen, the tone of voice to convey meaning and the body language used to reiterate both. It is heavily determined by social setting, context, purpose and audience. A person at a party would use their register differently from when they attend a meeting.

Polysemy

Some words have multiple meanings. Polysemy refers to one word that has two or more separate meanings. It is the opposite of *monosemy*, which refers to a word with one specific meaning.

Etymology

Words develop over time from their original state. Etymology tracks words back to their origin and studies their developments across history. It is particularly important when thinking about contextual and comprehension understanding of vocabulary.

While I am not advocating teaching Reception children all these terms, we must understand as practitioners what it means to *know* a word. Background knowledge is integral if we want to build a firm foundation for our pupils, and ultimately, that is what it is all about: giving our young people the best possible start. The learning that takes place around these terms is fundamental, and to facilitate that learning, it is our job to provide expert teaching and provision.

KEY TAKEAWAYS

- Words are the smallest unit of language that can be used independently.
- Understanding the complexities of language helps teachers to teach vocabulary effectively.

Breadth and Depth

There are around 170,000 words currently in use within the English language, which is by no means a small number. In a 2016 study analysing the results of one million test-takers, researchers determined that native English-speaking Americans know an average of at least 42,000 words by the time they are 20 years old (Brysbaert et al., 2016). Of course, I am not advocating that we attempt to teach 42,000 words to our little learners, but if we, as a wider profession, want to ensure a rich, robust vocabulary by the time a pupil leaves schooling, then that journey starts with us.

Here, it is essential to factor in that while recognising a wide range of words (breadth) is important, understanding (depth) also has a vital role. Securing both vocabulary breadth and depth (Nagy and Herman, 1987) is fundamental to complete vocabulary acquisition.

On top of this, a distinction should be made between knowing the 'meaning of words' in the context of oral language and the role that vocabulary plays in reading comprehension. There have been many crucial links made between oral and written language. Gough and Tunmer (1986) found that oral language, working in tandem with word reading, was integral for reading comprehension; this will not surprise teachers. We know that if children are familiar with the words in a sentence, they are far more likely to comprehend the sentence as a whole.

Though referring to older students, it is worth bearing in mind that Hirsch (2003) puts forward that 90–95 per cent word understanding when reading a text will still need additional support to fully comprehend it.

Oral vocabulary knowledge does not just help children comprehend a word they are reading; it also helps them to accurately read a written word when encountering it for the first time (McKague et al., 2001; Duff and Hulme, 2012).

KEY TAKEAWAYS

- The average adult knows around 42,000 words by the time they are 20 years old.
- Both breadth and depth are needed for full vocabulary acquisition (Nagy and Herman, 1987).
- Oral language is critical for developing both word reading and comprehension.

> **Pause for Reflection**
>
> Consider the profound impact of understanding the intricate layers of language on your approach to teaching vocabulary. How does your awareness of concepts like phonemes, morphemes, syntax and semantics shape the way you introduce and reinforce words in your classroom?

THE EARLY YEARS GAP

While there have been many pedagogical discussions surrounding vocabulary in recent times outside of the immediate community, Early Years is often forgotten. Those within our community know how important language is for our young learners. What starts as a vocabulary gap in Reception class can become something far more significant as the child moves through their education if it is not addressed quickly.

Think about your class. How many children started Reception lacking the necessary vocabulary to fully access learning? I imagine you can picture quite a few off the top of your head. I know I can. Government research published in the 2017 'Unlocking Talent, Fulfilling Potential' report states:

> 'By the age of three, more disadvantaged children are – on average – already almost a full year and a half behind their more affluent peers in their early language development. And around two fifths of disadvantaged five-year-olds are not meeting the expected literacy standard for their age.' (Department for Education, 2017: 11)

These are shocking statistics but unsurprising for anyone working in the Early Years. As already discussed, there are multiple links between social disadvantage and language deprivation. Social disadvantage is not the defining factor of poor language development, but it is a risk factor.

We also know that 1 in 10 children have speech, language and communication needs (SLCN) which can manifest in many ways (Speech and Language UK, n.d.) It can impact understanding of what others say and a child's social use of language, forming sounds and words and formulating sentences, among many other things. Crucially, it can have a pronounced impact on curriculum accessibility.

Many children enter Reception, communicating with only basic words and language. It automatically puts them at a disadvantage against their peers with more advanced vocabulary. As the year goes on, if this is not tackled, the vocabulary deficit becomes more pronounced and children will potentially be unable to access increasing elements of the curriculum because of their lack of understanding.

Due to the nature of our role, we are privileged to observe and know the children in our care closely. It means that we can address issues quickly. However, wouldn't it be wonderful to create an environment that anticipates these issues and has clear strategies, teaching and provision to tackle them before they become such? And not just for those children we can identify, but for all children because, as the evidence shows, an early vocabulary gap can have a lasting impact on a child's schooling life.

Research from Wasik and Bond (2001) shows that a whole-class vocabulary approach allows for successful vocabulary acquisition. While whole-class teaching can be a contentious issue for some in the early years, when appropriately delivered, we can provide high-quality learning experiences for our little learners that generate immediate exposure to language experiences. Not only is this immediate, but it is also equitable in ensuring that all children get access to the fundamentals.

Of course, this does not mean an overly formalised learning environment all the time, but rather explicit teaching in conjunction with play-based provision to ensure successful vocabulary acquisition. The very nature of vocabulary lends itself to explicit instruction, which Chapter 5 will discuss in more detail.

Undoubtedly, an enabling environment that provides opportunities for language to take place will contribute to this acquisition. However, knowing that when some children enter Reception, they are already at a deficit when compared with other children in their class, relying on it as the sole source is leaving too much to chance.

By starting this efficiently and, most importantly, *early*, we are giving children the best possible shot at narrowing the gap, and increasing and enhancing their vocabulary knowledge, building both their breadth and depth of vocabulary. By giving children this strong start, practitioners are laying secure foundations to lessen the chance of future issues.

KEY TAKEAWAYS

- Government research in 2017 found that by age 3, the average disadvantaged child is nearly 18 months behind in early language development.
- 1 in 10 children have speech, language and communication needs (SLCN).
- Whole-class vocabulary teaching is an efficient and equitable way of ensuring that all children are given fundamental language teaching.
- Direct teaching used in conjunction with play-based provision will ensure that successful vocabulary acquisition takes place.

> **Pause for Reflection**
>
> Consider the vocabulary levels in your Reception class against the backdrop of early language gaps. How do you support the vocabulary needs in your class, including those with speech, language and communication needs?

Fundamentals of Vocabulary Teaching in Reception

We know the *why*, but what about the *how*? So often, teachers are given research findings but without the necessary guidance to implement them effectively. Having the background knowledge plays an integral part, of course, but on top of this, we must build effective practice so our children can learn.

So what does that look like? Here are my fundamental principles for creating a vocabulary-rich environment that the following chapters of the book will be framed around.

Child-Centred Approach

Ultimately, our children should be what drives us as teachers. Everything we do should come back to them. EYFS is child-centred, and what I put forward in this book is no exception. By combining explicit teaching, play and environment, it is centred around the individual child's needs.

Class Culture

Words should be at the heart of everything in the Reception classroom. If this culture is carried throughout the school – even better! It can be one of the more complex areas to get right because there is no one big thing to implement that will immediately change the culture. Instead, it is an approach that requires many small steps that everyone in the class team must be on board with. In order to do this, you have to ensure buy-in from all of the members of the team. The aim is to create a vocabulary-enriched culture where all the adults in the room are motivated to help the children succeed in word acquisition.

Language should be everywhere: in the selected books, in the poetry performed to the class and talking about how the words are used within them. With research from the National Literacy Trust showing that 1 in 8 children in the North East do not own a single book (National Literacy Trust, 2017), book talk has never been more important.

Highlight the rhymes, the funny words, the gruesome, the silly and the adorable. Embody those words so the children can see how special you find them.

Make words of the week front and centre in the classroom. We all know how to perform in Early Years to be larger than life and engaging for our little learners. Use that to your advantage.

Take the words of the week and turn them into word celebrities so the children cannot help but be influenced by your enthusiasm and want to use them, too. Draw attention to the children using the words in their own language and make them feel like superstars.

Foundations First

As discussed earlier, limited vocabulary can have a marked impact on future learning opportunities, so it is integral that we build secure vocabulary foundations in order for more advanced vocabulary acquisition to take place. A child with a limited understanding and usage of positional language will undoubtedly be hindered in future maths learning. Teaching and embedding the required positional language can prevent that from taking place. Therefore, early targeting of fundamental vocabulary is integral into the curriculum from the beginning of Reception.

Strategic Word Selection

When considering word choices, teachers should ensure that they are selecting the correct vocabulary for their context. Choosing the right words is crucial in developing language. When choosing words, consider that words should be new for most of the cohort, yet chosen because they are likely to be repeatedly encountered throughout Reception and their early schooling. A good rule of thumb is to ask whether a child's development will be hindered without knowledge of a particular word. If the answer is yes, then teach them the word. We discuss this in more detail in Chapter 4.

The vocabulary chosen must be at an accessible level for Reception children. Teachers should also be aware of how many words they provide as we want to enthuse, not overwhelm children.

Be Explicit

Direct teaching has a vital part to play in Reception, particularly regarding vocabulary acquisition. For the very first time, we are introducing concepts to little minds that they have never encountered before. It is essential to do that with clarity so that no early misconceptions must be unpicked later on. Ensuring clear, precise teaching in a structured manner means that nothing is left to chance for each and every child. It can be done in both small groups and whole-class teaching.

Retrieval

One exposure to a word is simply not enough. In order to ensure that the word is embedded, it is necessary to have multiple exposures. To that end, it is imperative that children are given the opportunity to do so. Here is where vocabulary-based retrieval practice comes in. In its simplest form, retrieval is all about moving knowledge from short-term to long-term memory (Jones, 2019). We want the words to be easily accessible to our little learners so they can easily call upon them and use them seamlessly in their own language, and later in their reading and writing. For that to happen, time must be built into the day to develop an understanding of previously taught words.

Alongside this, ensure that selected words are those that children will have multiple exposures to outside teaching moments. Words that may appear in stories are read to them in media such as films or television shows, or in different areas of learning (positional language in maths). Give children the opportunity to use words independently. These exposures will help embed new vocabulary into their long-term memory.

Contextualise and Explore

A child's knowledge of a word will inevitably develop over time as exposure increases. It is important to contextualise the word as they are learning it to build depth and breadth. Exploring words can be really fun, and that should be translated to the children. If you are teaching the word 'pour', then pour liquid. When they are by the water tray, tell them they are pouring water. Ask them which jug they want to use next to pour more water. Make the word real and understandable for them.

Reception teachers have the perfect environment for this to happen. Early Years classrooms are ideal for physical contextualisation and exploration, which practitioners are exceptionally skilled at. The key is persistently using the language alongside the practical to draw links between the two.

Incorporate Play

Early Years and play go hand in hand. Play helps our children make sense of the world, so by incorporating vocabulary into play-based situations, we are helping them make sense of vocabulary. Teachers can both reinforce vocabulary and motivate children, as seen in Chapter 7.

KEY TAKEAWAYS

- Everything should be centred around the child's needs. This approach combines explicit teaching, play and an engaging environment.
- Develop a culture where vocabulary is at the core of all activities. Establishing solid vocabulary foundations early on is critical to enable advanced vocabulary learning later.
- Practise retrieval to move knowledge from short-term to long-term memory. Integrate vocabulary into play-based activities for contextual learning and reinforcement.

> **Pause for Reflection**
>
> In your classroom, how do you blend explicit vocabulary teaching with playful exploration? Reflect on how this combination enriches the children's vocabulary and shapes their overall learning experience.

THE GUIDE MODEL

The GUIDE approach is something I have used in Reception and Key Stage 1. It provides a clear, structured pathway to effective vocabulary instruction and is designed to help teachers ensure that every learner gets the support they need to flourish. The book will discuss it in detail as an integral method of explicitly teaching vocabulary. The acronym is intended to provide a streamlined, easily remembered set of principles for vocabulary teaching, underpinned by the theoretically robust foundations of Rosenshine's 'Principles of Instruction' (Rosenshine, 2012), as discussed in Chapter 3.

GUIDE stands for Gather, Unveil, Interact, Demonstrate, Embed. Each represents a key component of effective vocabulary instruction, from reviewing previously learned words to introducing new vocabulary, facilitating interactive practice, modelling correct usage and pronunciation, and embedding these words in daily routines for regular review. GUIDE is a simplified framework to help Early Years educators comprehensively structure their teaching.

KEY TAKEAWAYS

- Each GUIDE stage (Gather, Unveil, Interact, Demonstrate, Embed) represents a significant aspect of vocabulary instruction, from consolidating previously learned words, unveiling new words, interactive practice, modelling usage and pronunciation to embedding words in daily routines for constant review.

SUMMING UP

Many elements of understanding are needed to fully comprehend a word, including grammar, phonetics and phonemics, morphology, register, semantics, syntax, polysemy and etymology. Alongside this, factors of disadvantage, language barriers, and speech and language considerations make early vocabulary acquisition incredibly complex.

By weaving together the fundamentals of vocabulary acquisition, teachers can create the enabling elements that give Reception children not only a comprehensive understanding of words, but also a growing library of vocabulary at their disposal.

> **Pause for Reflection**
>
> What are you currently doing in your environment to support vocabulary acquisition?

AUDIT

Table 1.1 An Audit for Practitioners to Assess their Current Practice

Consider	Currently in Place	Next Steps
Can practitioners (including support staff) in your setting describe a child's stage of development in speech, language and communication?		
How is a child's vocabulary acquisition currently monitored?		
What strategies are currently in place to support vocabulary acquisition?		
How does the environment support a vocabulary-rich culture?		
What books are read to the children?		
How is play used to develop language?		
How do practitioners interact with children to develop language?		

2
DOES THE EYFS FRAMEWORK AND 'DEVELOPMENT MATTERS' GUIDE EFFECTIVE VOCABULARY TEACHING IN RECEPTION?

In this chapter, we will embark on a journey to understand the Early Years framework (Department for Education, 2021d, 2021e) and Development Matters (Department for Education, 2021f) and explore how they can be linked directly to the effective teaching of vocabulary in Reception.

It must be remembered that both the Early Years Foundation Stage (EYFS) and Development Matters cover the age range of 0–5 years. However, we will be focusing on how these documents affect Reception-aged children. To discuss these documents in their entirety would require a book in and of itself, as they encompass a wealth of information. Therefore, we will take a whistle-stop tour of them and examine how they relate to vocabulary acquisition in the Reception year.

I will demonstrate that teaching vocabulary in Reception can and should be approached through both established Early Years teaching methods and more traditional, explicit teaching methods. By understanding the guidance set out in these documents, we can ensure that both teaching approaches align with the best practices for promoting language acquisition and development in young children. By adopting a well-rounded approach to vocabulary teaching, we can support the development of a strong language foundation in our Reception-aged children.

STATUTORY FRAMEWORK FOR EYFS

In September 2021, The Early Years Foundation Stage (EYFS) reforms were implemented following trials and feedback from various schools and educational experts. These changes were driven by a desire to streamline the curriculum, prioritise child development and reduce the administrative burden on practitioners. The government listed one of the key reasons for reform as 'to improve outcomes at age 5, particularly in early language and especially for disadvantaged children' (Department for Education, 2021a). Despite their intent, the reforms have been met with both support and criticism.

While the spirited debates surrounding the EYFS reforms are indeed fascinating and warrant exploration, I must politely tip my hat to those discussions and step aside, for they fall beyond the purview of this chapter. Instead, I will direct my attention and yours to vocabulary development. As we delve into this captivating world, we leave the intricacies of the reforms to other capable hands, allowing us to embrace wholeheartedly the linguistic adventures that lie ahead.

When reflecting on the EYFS, speaking from a teacher's perspective, I can assure you that it transcends the mere concept of guidelines – it represents a philosophy of learning rooted in fundamental principles. At the heart of the EYFS is the recognition that every child is unique, and as teachers we need to understand and respond to each child's individual needs and abilities. It means taking the time to get to know each child. In essence, the EYFS cultivates a passion for learning and lays the groundwork for a lifetime of accomplishments.

All schools and Early Years providers who are Ofsted registered follow the EYFS. It does not just include Reception classes but also nurseries, preschools and private childminders. It gives practitioners the legal standards for developing, learning and caring for children from birth to 5 years old.

EYFS applies specifically to England. Both Scotland and Wales have different standards that can be found online. This chapter will focus solely on the EYFS framework, which, although legally used in England, is renowned worldwide for its focus on child-centred practice.

Teachers, middle leaders and senior leadership teams (SLTs) must possess a comprehensive understanding of both Development Matters and the EYFS framework to guarantee that children receive developmentally appropriate education tailored to their unique needs. Without this understanding, there is a risk of headteachers inadvertently transforming Reception Year into a mere replica of Key Stage 1 and beyond, an approach that does not align with the developmental needs of young children. Such a scenario could expose children to academic content beyond their developmental stage, which, as we know from our experience as teachers, can lead to disengagement, frustration and a negative attitude towards learning.

Nevertheless, explicit vocabulary teaching is essential in the Early Years. In order to ensure its effectiveness and appropriateness, it must be closely tied to the EYFS framework, allowing for developmentally suitable learning experiences.

KEY TAKEAWAYS

- In September 2021, reforms were made to the EYFS to streamline and prioritise child development and reduce the administrative burden on practitioners.
- These reforms were intended to improve outcomes at age 5, particularly in early language and especially for disadvantaged children.
- The EYFS framework is a learning philosophy rooted in fundamental principles, recognising that every child is unique.
- Teachers, middle leaders and senior leadership teams must possess a comprehensive understanding of both Development Matters and the EYFS framework to ensure that children receive developmentally appropriate education tailored to their needs.

> **Pause for Reflection**
>
> Consider how the EYFS reforms, emphasising early language and child development, shape your approach to vocabulary teaching in the Early Years. How do you ensure that your teaching strategies align with the EYFS framework?

Essential Principles of the Early Years Foundation Stage

To fully understand the framework, it first needs to be recognised that the entire Foundation Stage is centred around essential principles that are reflected throughout.

Every Child is a Unique Child, Who is Constantly Learning and can be Resilient, Capable, Confident and Self-Assured (Department for Education, 2021c)

The first principle highlights the importance of understanding that every child is unique, with their own individual strengths and areas of development. Teachers can use that information to create supportive learning environments that meet their specific requirements by understanding and responding to each child's needs. It means taking the time to get to know each child.

Research shows that children learn best when teaching is tailored to their individual needs and abilities (Dowling, 2018). When it comes to vocabulary, some children may need more support than others. For example, a child learning English as an additional language may need extra support to develop their vocabulary, whereas another child may need help to develop their language comprehension.

Understanding each child's individual needs and abilities is the foundation for effective vocabulary instruction. Teachers can tailor their instruction to meet their specific requirements by getting to know each child. It can involve providing – alongside and within vocabulary lessons – additional support or scaffolding for children who need it or providing opportunities for more advanced learners to extend their vocabulary.

In addition, when teachers recognise and value each child's individual strengths, they can help to foster their confidence and self-assurance. Children who feel confident and self-assured are more likely to engage in the learning process actively and take risks with new vocabulary (Hughes, 2009). Creating an environment where children feel safe to experiment with new words and ask questions is essential as a teacher. Relationships are vital in creating that environment.

Children Learn to be Strong and Independent Through Positive Relationships (Department for Education, 2021c).

The second principle is all about relationships. It is of the utmost importance that children feel secure and valued, and building positive relationships with their teachers and caregivers is crucial. As a teacher, you must create a welcoming environment conducive to building relationships. Research has shown that children who have positive relationships with their teachers are more likely to actively engage in the learning process. Hamre and Pianta (2001) found that positive teacher–student relationships in the Early Years can lead to better academic outcomes, improved social–emotional development and better mental health in later years.

Take the time to really get to know them as little human beings. Who are their favourite superheroes? What are their favourite books to read? What is the best food in the world? What is the scariest dinosaur? What kind of games do they like to play? Get to know their family backgrounds and their culture. Find ways to engage with their parents or carers and encourage them to be involved in their child's learning journey. All of this is going to set the groundwork for the teaching of vocabulary. With those relationships in place, it becomes much easier for learning to happen.

Children Learn and Develop Well in Enabling Environments, in Which their Experiences Respond to their Individual Needs and There is a Strong Partnership Between Practitioners and Parents and/or Carers (Department for Education, 2021c).

The third principle is all about creating an enabling environment. Children learn best when they have access to various resources, materials and experiences tailored to their needs. Teachers can support children's development and encourage a love of learning by designing a rich and stimulating learning environment that responds to children's interests and abilities.

An enabling environment in Early Years provision involves creating a physically and emotionally supportive space. It means providing a range of resources, materials and activities tailored to children's needs and interests. For example, a classroom may include areas for quiet reading, messy play, construction and role-playing.

When it comes to the explicit teaching of vocabulary, alongside the teaching, the environment is a crucial component in backing up and furthering the teaching. A study by Sammons et al. (2004) found that the quality of the Early Years environment significantly impacts children's language development. Providing a rich and stimulating learning environment with resources and materials tailored to children's needs can lead to better language outcomes in the long term.

One of the critical aspects of creating an enabling environment for vocabulary development is to ensure that children have access to a range of resources and materials that support the explicit teaching of vocabulary. Teachers can support children's language development by creating a rich and stimulating learning environment that promotes vocabulary development.

In addition to the physical environment and activities, adults play a crucial role in creating an enabling environment in Early Years provision. Hearing and engaging with those taught words being spoken in context is fundamental in ensuring that the word is remembered and used independently by the child.

While the exact number of times a child needs to hear and use a word to store it in their long-term memory can vary, research has shown that active engagement with a word through multiple encounters and meaningful contexts is essential for learning and retaining it in long-term memory. A study by Carey et al. (2019) found that repetition is not only important for learning words, but also for the quality and depth of the child's engagement with the word. Children need to use the word in different contexts and with different meanings to gain a deeper understanding of its meaning and to store it in long-term memory. We will look at this in closer detail in Chapter 3.

Children Develop and Learn in Different Ways and at Different Rates (Department for Education, 2021c).

Finally, the fourth principle emphasises the importance of inclusivity. Every child learns in their own unique way, and it is essential to ensure that all children have access to high-quality education, regardless of their individual needs or abilities. By providing inclusive education that meets the needs of all children, teachers can help to promote equality and ensure that every child has the opportunity to achieve their full potential.

When it comes to vocabulary development in Reception class, inclusivity means considering the needs of children who may be learning English as an additional language or those with special educational needs. Baker et al. (2014) found that children with special educational needs who were provided with individualised support made significant progress in their language development.

Here, quality-first teaching comes in alongside careful use of assessment and consideration of the specific needs of *your* cohort. When it comes to teaching vocabulary in Reception class, small group teaching is a great way to focus more fully on individual children's needs. It allows teachers to provide more personalised support and adapt their teaching strategies to meet the needs of each child.

Another way to ensure inclusivity is to use the pre-teaching strategy. We all know that every child is unique and learns at their own pace. Some children may require more time and support to learn new concepts, which is totally okay. As teachers, it is our job to provide support to help all children succeed.

Here is where pre-teaching comes in. Introducing key vocabulary words to children before they encounter them in their reading or other activities can give them a head start and help them feel more confident in their ability to understand and use the new words.

Pre-teaching is particularly helpful for children who may be learning English as an additional language or may have special educational needs. By providing extra support and opportunities for practice, we can ensure that all children have the opportunity to learn and develop their vocabulary in a way that is appropriate for their individual needs and abilities.

KEY TAKEAWAYS

- Effective vocabulary instruction requires understanding and responding to each child's individual needs and abilities.
- Building positive relationships with students and caregivers is crucial for creating a safe and supportive learning environment that fosters confidence and self-assurance.
- Creating an enabling environment that responds to children's interests and abilities is key to promoting vocabulary development and encouraging a love of learning.
- Hearing and engaging with taught words in context is essential in ensuring that children remember and use words independently.
- Pre-teaching key vocabulary words to children before encountering them in reading or other activities can help give them a head start and make them feel more confident in their ability to understand and use the new words.

> **Pause for Reflection**
>
> Consider how your classroom environment, both physical and emotional, serves as an enabling space for vocabulary acquisition. How do you ensure inclusivity in your approach, addressing your students' diverse learning needs?

AREAS OF LEARNING

So, now the essential principles of EYFS are out of the way, next comes Areas of Learning. The Areas of Development in the Early Years is a vital component of EYFS. It is key to understand that all areas are interconnected and should be considered equally crucial within the phase.

The document identifies three **prime areas** of development: *Communication and Language, Physical Development,* and *Personal, Social and Emotional Development.* These areas are the building blocks for all learning and development and are essential for children's well-being and future success. These areas lay the groundwork for success in all other aspects of the curriculum, and they are particularly crucial for young children's emotional, cognitive and physical growth. Everything begins with the prime areas. (Department for Education, 2021c).

The framework also outlines four **specific areas** of development: *Literacy, Mathematics, Understanding the World,* and *Expressive Arts and Design.* The specific areas build upon the prime areas and are designed to provide more targeted and focused learning opportunities, further developing children's abilities in various aspects of learning.

Table 2.1 The Areas of Learning and Development from the Early Years Foundation Stage Statutory Framework for Group and School-Based Providers (DfE, 2021c)

	Area of Learning
Prime	1. Personal, Social and Emotional Development
	2. Communication and Language
	3. Physical Development
Specific	4. Literacy
	5. Mathematics
	6. Understanding the World
	7. Expressive Art and Design

The division of the Areas of Learning into prime and specific ensures a comprehensive and balanced approach to early education. The prime areas establish a strong foundation, while the specific areas further refine and expand children's knowledge and abilities. This cohesive structure underpins the entire Early Years curriculum. While all the areas of learning should, of course, be interwoven and overlap, some do lend themselves more naturally to the teaching of explicit vocabulary.

The Communication and Language statement specifically tells practitioners:

> The development of children's spoken language underpins all seven areas of learning and development. Children's back-and-forth interactions from an early age form the foundations for language and cognitive development. The number and quality of the conversations they have with adults and peers throughout the day in a language-rich environment is crucial. By commenting on what children are interested in or doing and echoing back what they say with new vocabulary added, practitioners will build children's language effectively. Reading frequently to children, engaging them actively in stories, non-fiction, rhymes and poems, and then providing them with extensive opportunities to use and embed new words in various contexts will allow children to thrive. Through conversation, story-telling and role play, where children share their ideas with support and modelling from their teacher, and sensitive questioning that invites them to elaborate, children become comfortable using a rich range of vocabulary and language structures. (DfE, 2021c)

To me, the framework could not be clearer in its support of the teaching of explicit vocabulary in Reception class through structured lessons as it recognises that children's language acquisition is bolstered through rich and diverse interactions, exposure to a wide range of vocabulary and active engagement in various language activities (DfE, 2021c).

Here are some ways that explicit vocabulary teaching is supported by the statutory guidance.

High-Quality Conversations

Explicit vocabulary instruction allows teachers to facilitate high-quality conversations with children. By actively introducing new words and language structures, teachers can stimulate children's curiosity and interest, encouraging them to participate in conversations and further develop their language skills.

Vocabulary Enrichment

Intentional vocabulary teaching exposes children to a broader range of words and phrases than they will encounter in everyday conversations. This exposure is vital in helping young children build a strong vocabulary foundation.

Active Engagement in Language Activities

The EYFS framework highlights the importance of engaging children in stories, non-fiction, rhymes and poems. Through explicit vocabulary lessons – some of which may be planned around the language in class stories – teachers can ensure that children are not only listening to these language-rich materials and actively participating, but are understanding and using the newly introduced words in various contexts. (DfE, 2021c). This active engagement helps children internalise and retain the new vocabulary.

Support and Modelling from Teachers

Explicit vocabulary instruction allows teachers to provide support and modelling to children as they learn new words. Teachers can guide children in constructing meaningful sentences and expressing their ideas effectively by providing clear examples and explanations with children echoing and using vocabulary in context. We will discuss this more in Chapter 5.

Role-Play and Storytelling

The EYFS framework emphasises the importance of role-play and storytelling in developing children's language abilities. (DfE, 2021c). As Early Year practitioners, we know that play is fundamental and, as has already been stated, I am in no way suggesting that it should be removed from the Early Years repertoire; instead, it should be utilised. The vocabulary that has been taught can be incorporated into both role-play and storytelling, allowing the opportunity to practise using new words and language structures in a playful way.

Confidence and Fluency

By teaching explicit vocabulary in Reception class and thus introducing a variety of new words, we allow children to become more comfortable using a rich range of vocabulary in various contexts. Children must regularly use vocabulary in order for it to be transferred into their long-term memory. The assertion that children must regularly use vocabulary for it to be transferred into their long-term memory is well supported by research in cognitive psychology and language development (Golinkoff and Hirsh-Pasek, 2006).

Let us consider the Literacy Area of Learning:

> It is crucial for children to develop a lifelong love of reading. Reading consists of two dimensions: language comprehension and word reading. Language comprehension (necessary for both reading and writing) starts from birth. It only develops when adults talk with children about the world around them and the books (stories and non-fiction) they read with them, and enjoy rhymes, poems and songs together. Skilled word reading, taught later, involves both the speedy working out of the pronunciation of unfamiliar printed words (decoding) and the speedy recognition of familiar printed words. Writing involves transcription (spelling and handwriting) and composition (articulating ideas and structuring them in speech, before writing). (DfE, 2021c)

Language comprehension is a key component. Let us look, then, at how Literacy aligns with the explicit teaching of vocabulary.

Language Comprehension

The EYFS framework acknowledges that language comprehension, a crucial aspect of reading and writing, begins at birth (DfE, 2021c). Teaching explicit vocabulary helps enhance children's understanding of texts by introducing them to new words and phrases, allowing them to make sense of the stories, non-fiction materials, poems, and songs they encounter.

Adult–Child Interactions

The EYFS strongly emphasises the value of adults talking with children about the world around them and the books they read together (DfE, 2021c). Explicit vocabulary lessons enable teachers to engage in rich conversations with children about new words, their meanings and their usage in various contexts. These interactions facilitate children's language development and deepen their understanding of the texts they explore. We must give children the opportunity to have these rich discussions, but without the tool of vocabulary, the discussion is limited.

Vocabulary is not just limited to these areas either. PSED (Personal, Social and Emotional Development) states: 'Children should be supported to manage emotions' (DfE, 2021c). In order to fully understand and manage emotion, children have to know the language of emotion itself. Without this articulation, it is hard to manage emotion.

In Understanding the World, we are told:

> Listening to a broad selection of stories, non-fiction, rhymes and poems will foster their understanding of our culturally, socially, technologically and ecologically diverse world. As well as building important knowledge, this extends their familiarity with words that support understanding across domains. Enriching and widening children's vocabulary will support later reading comprehension. (DfE, 2021c)

The framework recognises that enriching and widening children's vocabulary builds crucial knowledge and supports their later reading comprehension. Yet again we see the acknowledgement that a rich vocabulary is key to children's overall development and understanding of the world around them.

Ultimately, the Areas of Learning emphasise the importance of vocabulary in young children's lives. By embedding vocabulary development throughout, the framework ensures that children have the necessary communication skills to flourish academically, emotionally and socially throughout their early educational journey.

KEY TAKEAWAYS

- The EYFS framework outlines two categories of development areas: prime and specific Areas of Learning. These interconnected areas ensure a comprehensive and balanced approach to early education.

- The development of children's spoken language is crucial to all seven areas of learning and development.
- Explicit vocabulary teaching benefits children by providing high-quality conversations, vocabulary enrichment, active engagement in language activities, support and modelling from teachers, opportunities for role-play and storytelling, and improved confidence and fluency in using a wide range of vocabulary.

> **Pause for Reflection**
>
> Consider the interconnectedness of the prime and specific Areas of Learning in the EYFS and how this impacts your approach to vocabulary development in your class. How do you weave vocabulary teaching into each area, ensuring that it aligns with the EYFS's emphasis on child-centred learning and holistic development? Consider the role of explicit vocabulary instruction in fostering language comprehension, enriching conversations and enhancing children's emotional and social understanding.

EARLY LEARNING GOALS

First things first: it is important to understand that the Early Learning Goals (ELG) should not be seen as a curriculum or restrict the range of experiences that are essential for a child's growth and development. Instead, they provide a set of expectations for what children should know and be able to do by the end of Reception (DfE, 2021c)

As teachers, our role is to use our expert professional judgement and knowledge of each child to make a holistic assessment of their progress against the 17 ELGs, which are divided into seven Areas of Learning. Early Years practitioners should observe and assess children's skills and abilities across all seven Areas of Learning and Development outlined in the ELGs.

Importantly, there is no need for formal documentation or evidence-gathering to assess children's progress against the ELGs. Instead, we can draw on our observations, interactions and knowledge of each child to make a judgement about their overall development.

Recognising vocabulary's pivotal role within the EYFS framework is crucial, as evidenced by its mention and assessment across the 17 Early Learning Goals. Early Learning Goals should not be perceived as a rigid set of teaching criteria, but rather as a collection of clear expectations that children should strive to attain by the end of their Early Years journey (of course, this would not be the case for children with specific SEND needs). The ELGs, and indeed, the entire EYFS acknowledge the enormous importance of vocabulary development.

Table 2.2 The Prime Areas Early Learning Goals taken from the Early Years Foundation Stage Statutory Framework for Group and School-Based Providers (DfE, 2021c)

Prime Areas		
Communication and Language	Personal, Social and Emotional Development	Physical Development
Listening and attention Children listen attentively in a range of situations. They listen to stories, accurately anticipating key events and respond to what they hear with relevant comments, questions or actions. They give their attention to what others say and respond appropriately, while engaged in another activity. **Understanding** Children follow instructions involving several ideas or actions. They answer 'how' and 'why' questions about their experiences and in response to stories or events. **Speaking** Children express themselves effectively, showing awareness of listeners' needs. They use past, present and future forms accurately when talking about events that have happened or are to happen in the future. They develop their own narratives and explanations by connecting ideas or events.	**Self-confidence and self-awareness** Children are confident to try new activities and say why they like some activities more than others. They are confident to speak in a familiar group, will talk about their ideas, and will choose the resources they need for their chosen activities. They say when they do or don't need help. **Managing feelings and behaviour** Children talk about how they and others show feelings, talk about their own and others' behaviour, and its consequences, and know that some behaviour is unacceptable. They work as part of a group or class, and understand and follow the rules. They adjust their behaviour to different situations and take changes of routine in their stride. **Making relationships** Children play co-operatively, taking turns with others. They take account of one another's ideas about how to organise their activity. They show sensitivity to others' needs and feelings, and form positive relationships with adults and other children.	**Moving and handling** Children show good control and co-ordination in large and small movements. They move confidently in a range of ways, safely negotiating space. They handle equipment and tools effectively, including pencils for writing. **Health and self-care** Children know the importance of physical exercise and a healthy diet for good health, and talk about ways to keep healthy and safe. They manage their own basic hygiene and personal needs successfully, including dressing and going to the toilet independently.

Table 2.3 The Specific Areas Early Learning Goals taken from the Early Years Foundation Stage Statutory Framework for Group and School-Based Providers (DfE, 2021)

		Specific Areas	
Literacy	Mathematics	Understanding the World	Expressive Arts and Design
Reading Children read and understand simple sentences. They use phonic knowledge to decode regular words and read them aloud accurately. They also read some common irregular words. They demonstrate understanding when talking with others about what they have read. **Writing** Children use their phonic knowledge to write words in ways that match their spoken sounds. They also write some irregular common words. They write simple sentences which can be read by themselves and others. Some words are spelt correctly and others are phonetically plausible.	**Numbers** Children count reliably with numbers from 1 to 20, place them in order and say which number is one more or one less than a given number. Using quantities and objects, they add and subtract two single-digit numbers and count on or back to find the answer. They solve problems, including doubling, halving and sharing. **Shape, space and measures** Children use everyday language to talk about size, weight, capacity, position, distance, time and money to compare quantities and objects and to solve problems. They recognise, create and describe patterns. They explore characteristics of everyday objects and shapes, and use mathematical language to describe them.	**People and communities** Children talk about past and present events in their own lives and in the lives of family members. They know that other children don't always enjoy the same things and are sensitive to this. They know about similarities and differences between themselves and others, and among families, communities and traditions. **The world** Children know about similarities and differences in relation to places, objects, materials and living things. They talk about the features of their own immediate environment and how environments might vary from one another. They make observations of animals and plants, explain why some things occur and talk about changes. **Technology** Children recognise that a range of technology is used in places such as homes and schools. They select and use technology for particular purposes.	**Exploring and using media and materials** Children sing songs, make music and dance, and experiment with ways of changing them. They safely use and explore a variety of materials, tools and techniques, experimenting with colour, design, texture, form and function. **Being imaginative** Children use what they have learnt about media and materials in original ways, thinking about uses and purposes. They represent their own ideas, thoughts and feelings through design and technology, art, music, dance, role-play and stories.

KEY TAKEAWAYS

- Early Learning Goals (ELGs) should not be viewed as a curriculum or restrictive; instead, they are a set of expectations for children by the end of Reception (DfE, 2021c)
- Teachers use their professional judgement to assess children's progress against the 17 ELGs, divided into seven Areas of Learning.
- Vocabulary plays a pivotal role within the EYFS framework, with its importance acknowledged across the 17 Early Learning Goals.

DEVELOPMENT MATTERS

Development Matters (Department for Education, 2021) is a guidance resource specifically crafted to assist Early Years practitioners in England with implementing the revised EYFS framework.

Development Matters, though a non-statutory guidance document, is widely used by the majority of Early Years practitioners in England due to its comprehensive approach to children's learning and development, as well as its research-based pedagogical foundation. The document provides practical strategies, suggestions and examples that support educators in creating effective learning environments while allowing for flexibility and adaptability to suit each unique context.

As with the EYFS framework, we will be discussing Development Matters within the context of Reception class while being mindful that the document covers the ages range of 0–5 years old.

Pause for Reflection

Consider how your observations and interactions with each child inform your judgement of their progress in vocabulary development. How do you balance the need for holistic development with the specific focus on vocabulary, ensuring that children are not just meeting but thriving within these learning goals? Reflect on the importance of recognising each child's unique journey, especially those with specific SEND needs, in achieving these goals.

CHARACTERISTICS OF EFFECTIVE LEARNING

As Early Years practitioners, we place the individual child at the heart of everything we do. The Characteristics of Effective Teaching and Learning (Department for Education, 2021b) are seen as a fundamental part of that. They have been part of Development Matters since 2012 and, although not statutory, are integral to Early Years.

Table 2.4 Descriptors of the Characteristics of Effective Teaching and Learning taken from Development Matters (Department for Education, 2021b)

Characteristic	Descriptor
Playing and exploring	Children investigate and experience things, and 'have a go'.
Active learning	Children concentrate and keep on trying if they encounter difficulties, and enjoy their achievements.
Creating and thinking critically	Children have and develop their own ideas, make links between ideas and develop strategies for doing things.

You have probably heard some Early Years practitioners passionately advocate for the power of play, suggesting that the Characteristics of Effective Learning (CoEL) are the ultimate proof of its importance. They argue that these principles demonstrate how play should take centre stage in Early Years education, and that explicit and direct teaching shouldn't be a top priority. They lean on research, like that conducted by Whitebread et al. (2012), which emphasises the critical role of play in children's cognitive, social and emotional development.

I don't dispute the power of play. As mentioned throughout this book, play is very important and no Reception class should be without it. Indeed, a whole chapter of the book (Chapter 8) discusses how to use play to our advantage when teaching vocabulary. However, for reasons already outlined, we must also ensure that explicit teaching is a vital part of our practice, and we can use CoEL to help us do that.

I like to think of it as a way to guide and support their learning journey. We cannot leave everything up to independent discovery. It is all about striking that balance. Of course, there are concerns about imposing adult goals onto a child's learning experience. However, when done thoughtfully and in line with a child's developmental stage and with a child-centred approach entirely in mind, direct teaching can actually enhance their curiosity and self-confidence.

Let us delve deeper into how these characteristics can harmoniously coexist with structured learning, particularly when it comes to vocabulary acquisition.

First, let us consider **playing and exploring**. While children are naturally inclined to investigate and experience their surroundings, direct teaching of new words facilitates their exploration of language's vast landscape. 'Having a go' with new words independently after they have been taught, is of equal importance to having a go in other areas, particularly when 'making independent choices', which is highlighted as one of the characteristics of 'having a go' in CoEL (Department for Education, 2021b).

Furthermore, incorporating the newly taught vocabulary into role-play scenarios, another CoEL characteristic (Department for Education, 2021b) can help children practise using the words in context, enriching their understanding and promoting the development of their social and emotional skills (Pellegrini and Galda, 1993). By integrating language learning with imaginative play, children can internalise new vocabulary more effectively while fostering creativity and collaboration.

Next is **active learning**. As children are introduced to new vocabulary through direct teaching, they are challenged to concentrate and persevere in understanding and utilising these fresh terms.

Lastly, we have **creating and thinking critically**. When children receive direct vocabulary instruction, they are equipped to develop their own ideas and forge connections between diverse concepts (Beck et al., 2002). By learning and internalising new words, they are empowered to apply them in various scenarios, honing their critical thinking skills and strategising their communication efforts.

To fully support this creative and critical thinking process, language education must be designed to facilitate it. As children acquire more knowledge and expand their vocabulary, they gain confidence in generating their ideas and making connections between them.

Having enhanced self-assurance, stemming from the CoEL characteristic of 'know more, so feel confident about coming up with their own ideas' (Department for Education, 2021b) enables them to explore new perspectives, think critically and communicate their thoughts more effectively.

KEY TAKEAWAYS

- Development Matters is non-statutory guidance for Early Years practitioners in England implementing the EYFS framework.
- The Characteristics of Effective Learning place the individual child at the heart of everything.
- Characteristics of Effective Learning can harmoniously coexist with structured learning, particularly when it comes to vocabulary acquisition.

Pause for Reflection

How do you balance the enriching power of play and exploration with the necessity of direct vocabulary instruction? Consider how introducing new words can enhance children's active learning and critical thinking, fostering both independence and a deeper understanding of language. Reflect on ways to support children in creating and thinking critically through enriched vocabulary experiences, nurturing their confidence and ability to communicate their ideas effectively.

SUMMING UP

Early Years teaching methods are, of course, crucial for engaging children in learning and fostering a love of language. However, we also need to recognise the importance of explicit teaching methods when it comes to vocabulary instruction. Children need direct instruction and explicit guidance to fully understand new words and their meanings.

By combining Early Years teaching methods with traditional, explicit teaching methods, we can also ensure that our teaching approaches are responsive to each child's individual needs and abilities, as well as create a well-rounded approach that aligns with the best practices for promoting language acquisition and development in young children.

Table 2.5 An Action Plan for Practitioners to Assess their Current Practice and Consider their Next Steps in order to Successfully Implement the Actions of Chapter 2

Action	Currently in Place	Next Steps
Familiarise yourself thoroughly with the EYFS framework's principles.		
Organise regular CPD for all relevant staff on the EYFS framework and Development Matters, focusing on vocabulary development. Include practical sessions on integrating vocabulary teaching into various areas of learning.		
Develop and distribute resource packs summarising key points of the EYFS and Development Matters, specifically related to vocabulary teaching.		
Schedule regular team meetings to discuss implementation of vocabulary teaching strategies. Use these meetings to share successes, challenges and brainstorm solutions.		

3
HOW DO CHILDREN LEARN?

In this chapter, we will explore the fascinating interconnections among Geary's (2005) research on biologically primary and secondary knowledge, Rosenshine's Principles (2012) and Cognitive Load Theory (Van Merriënboer and Sweller, 2005) – all crucial elements that contribute to the way we understand and enhance vocabulary acquisition in our young learners. I will examine these concepts and unveil their implications for early education.

First, we will dive into Geary's ground-breaking research framework on biologically primary and secondary knowledge. You will discover how these distinct types of knowledge are formed and why Geary's insights, though undeniably important, cannot be applied explicitly to Early Years as young learners are still developing their cognitive abilities. This understanding will shed light on the unique challenges faced by educators in the Early Years and guide you in tailoring teaching strategies accordingly.

Next, I will introduce you to Rosenshine's Principles, a set of research-based guidelines that can be invaluable in structuring Early Years education in an age-appropriate way. You will learn how these principles can be adapted to support young learners' cognitive and language development while keeping their needs in mind. I will demonstrate how these principles can seamlessly integrate into your teaching practices to create a purposeful and engaging learning environment.

We will then explore Cognitive Load Theory, a vital aspect of understanding of how children's minds process and retain new information. By comprehending the delicate balance of cognitive load in young learners, you will be better equipped to optimise learning experiences and ensure that your pupils can successfully absorb and apply new knowledge.

By examining these real-life examples alongside some top tips for the classroom, you will gain insights into the effectiveness of these approaches and, I hope, gather inspiration for your teaching practice.

When I was young, my parents separated. My childhood was spent primarily with my mum and little brother. We were not a well-off family and, as I grew older, it became very obvious as hardships became more apparent. I still distinctly remember the moment it dawned on me in Year 4 that education would become my ticket to a brighter future.

I love my family fiercely and have always been very family-orientated. Still, I longed for a life where money was not front and centre of our anxieties at all times, where the fridge was packed and the heating was on – the house toasty and inviting.

As fate would have it, my dad's business eventually took off and those worries faded from my mind. Nevertheless, the memories will remain etched in my heart for the rest of my life. I can still recall my intense desperation at eleven, knowing that passing my eleven-plus exam could change my life's trajectory (see below). Because of this high-stakes testing, I am not a fan of the eleven-plus system in Kent, but that is a story for another book.

We must make education count. It is often said that knowledge is power, but what is equally important is understanding how we acquire that knowledge in the first place. We must ensure that our pupils' learning truly counts by delving into the inner workings of the human mind to understand our cognitive processes.

It is for this reason that the theories discussed in this chapter – particularly Rosenshine's Principles and Cognitive Load Theory – resonate so deeply with me as a teacher of Reception (and Key Stage 1 children). These theories mean that nothing is left to chance and we ensure that no child gets left behind.

The Eleven-Plus System

The eleven-plus system is an exam that some children take when they are 11, which can determine whether they will attend a selective or grammar school. While many areas have abolished the eleven-plus for state schools, some local authorities, like Bucks and Kent, still have grammar schools and conduct county-wide entrance tests. A few grammar schools exist alongside the comprehensive system in other areas, like Barnet and Kingston. These schools set their entrance exams and select their pupils based on their performance in the eleven-plus exam.

The eleven-plus system has been criticised for its potential to create a two-tier education system, leaving other local schools without the highest-performing pupils. Additionally, children who do not do well in the exam at age 11 can be labelled as 'failures', which can be detrimental to their self-esteem and future academic performance.

GEARY'S FRAMEWORK

As we grow up, playtime is more than just fun and games; it can also be how we learn. This kind of learning is what Geary calls 'biologically primary knowledge', and he delves deep into this topic in his book *The Origin of Mind* (2005). Before we delve any deeper, it is important to caveat this section by bearing in mind that these ideas form the framework of an approach from Geary; it is crucial to recognise that his research on biologically primary and secondary knowledge is a theoretical lens rather than an absolute fact. While some elements make sense to me, there are other parts that I disagree with, as you will see.

Over time, our bodies and brains have adapted to various factors like the weather, the food we eat and even how we interact with each other. Geary believes that social interaction has significantly shaped our brains because it helps us access more resources.

Geary posits that due to these environmental pressures, our brains have developed special sections, or 'modules', that focus on processing specific types of information like language or recognising faces. These modules work quickly, without us even realising it, and help us form our 'go-to' patterns of thinking when it comes to understanding people, the natural world and physical objects (Geary, 2005).

But here is the exciting thing – we are not limited to these default ways of thinking. Our brains have flexible areas, particularly in the frontal regions, that allow us to think beyond these ingrained patterns. Geary calls the thinking that relies on these evolved modules 'biologically primary', while the more flexible, adaptable thought processes are 'biologically secondary'.

Geary breaks down biologically primary learning into several vital components. First, there's folk biology, which enables us to understand other species and our natural environment. Next comes folk psychology, responsible for our capacity to interact, cooperate and forge social connections with others. Lastly, folk physics allows us to grasp the physical world and manipulate objects to our advantage. Through play, we learn to understand other species (folk biology), interact and cooperate with others (folk psychology) and navigate the world of inanimate objects (folk physics). It is a crucial stage in a child's development (Geary, 2005).

Then there is 'biologically secondary' knowledge. Nature has also endowed our brains with the incredible ability to adapt and acquire new information that stems from our culture. This cultural information can be rather beneficial to us. However, the caveat is that it does not come as effortlessly as biologically primary knowledge is generally perceived to. In this sense, we move from basic learning to more complex learning.

Examples of biologically secondary knowledge include learning to read and write, solving complex maths problems or even understanding historical events.

These skills are developed through education, practice and cultural and environmental exposure.

It is where EYFS practitioners might find themselves at odds with other educators who work with older children. We often hear that these skills come naturally to us as we have evolved to learn them. While it is true that biologically primary knowledge is something we have developed to acquire, it is essential to remember that young children are still in the process of learning these skills when they attend their Early Years setting. Furthermore, let's remember that EYFS covers ages 0–5 years.

In addition, it is essential to note that what Geary calls 'biologically primary learning' may not come as instinctively to all children, given the evidence stated in Chapter 1. As a result, focusing on biologically primary areas becomes even more crucial for Early Years education, especially when considering vocabulary acquisition.

Weisleder and Fernald (2013) emphasise the importance of caregiver–child verbal interactions for strengthening language-processing skills and building vocabulary when considering language development in the home setting. Although children are predisposed to learn language, the study suggests that high-quality language input during early childhood is still essential for optimal language development.

Similarly, Hirsh-Pasek et al. (2015) investigate the impact of communication quality on language development in children from low-income families. Their findings underscore the role of high-quality, responsive communication with children in fostering language growth, even in the context of biologically primary knowledge.

Even though both of these studies primarily examine vocabulary acquisition within the home environment, the key takeaway remains clear: engaging in intentional language interactions and instruction is crucial for children to learn vocabulary most effectively.

At this stage in our exploration of the EYFS curriculum, it is clear that I am hesitant about depending entirely on play-based learning for specific areas. My perspective here might differ from that of other educators in the field. However, this should not be misconstrued as a dismissal of the value of play in early childhood education. The importance of play is discussed in detail in Chapter 8. When considering the statistics referenced in Chapter 1, a combination of explicit teaching and purposeful play is essential to ensure that children develop appropriately during their early years and combat these issues.

Our young children are not innately learning these biologically primary skills and we need to help them get there.

We must pay special attention to these biologically primary areas and employ teaching methods that incorporate direct, explicit instruction and purposeful play. This balanced approach helps children develop a strong foundation for future learning.

KEY TAKEAWAYS

- Playtime can help children develop biologically primary knowledge, which includes folk biology, folk psychology and folk physics.
- Some children do not innately gain biologically primary knowledge through play and need structured help to achieve this knowledge.
- Biologically secondary knowledge, such as reading and writing, is learned through education and exposure to culture and environment.
- Early Years education should focus on both biologically primary and secondary learning, combining explicit teaching with purposeful play for a well-rounded foundation.

> **Pause for Reflection**
>
> How can you provide high-quality, responsive communication and interactions for children from diverse backgrounds and abilities to optimise their language development and learning experiences in Early Years education?

ROSENSHINE'S PRINCIPLES

As fellow educators, we have all encountered different methods and pedagogies throughout our teaching journey. One of the methods that has gained traction and popularity in recent years is Rosenshine's Principles of Instruction (Rosenshine, 2012). Despite its massive popularity in education generally, there is a lingering debate about the appropriateness of these principles for Early Years education. Some critics argue that they are not developmentally suitable for young children, while others passionately endorse their use.

Table 3.1 Rosenshine's Principles (Rosenshine, 2012)

Rosenshine's Principles
1. Begin a lesson with a short review of previous learning.
2. Present new material in small steps with pupil practice after each step.
3. Ask a large number of questions and check the responses of all pupils.
4. Provide models.
5. Guide pupil practice.
6. Check for pupil understanding.
7. Obtain a high success rate.
8. Provide scaffolds for complex tasks.
9. Require and monitor independent practice.
10. Engage pupils in a weekly and monthly review.

Rosenshine's Principles of Instruction originated in the 1970s and were refined over the years (Rosenshine, 2012). These principles outline ten research-based instructional strategies that effectively improve pupil achievement. They include review, questioning, modelling, practice and monitoring pupil progress.

Now, I would argue that the principles are fundamentally good practices for ensuring the best possible learning for children. I understand the concerns about the developmental appropriateness of Rosenshine's principles for young children. Young learners have unique cognitive, social and emotional needs that differ from older pupils (Vygotsky, 1978).

Nevertheless, as discussed, focusing on nurturing curiosity, creativity and social–emotional development should not be discouraged. There is a time and a place for everything, and there is a place to use Rosenshine's Principles to underpin elements of Early Years learning. I myself use them often as the foundation on which to base many of my explicit teaching lessons within Reception, particularly in maths, phonics and vocabulary acquisition.

Rosenshine's principles can be adapted and integrated thoughtfully into Early Years education without sacrificing these developmental needs. The following are a few examples of what I use in my practice.

Review and questioning Reviewing prior knowledge helps children build a strong foundation for new learning. Questioning is a crucial part of any teacher's arsenal, which is no different in Early Years.

Modelling Modelling is essential for young children. By demonstrating how to approach a task, we provide a scaffold for their learning, ensuring that they develop the necessary skills and understandings in a supportive environment.

Practice and feedback Repeated practice is crucial for consolidating learning. In Early Years education, we can facilitate meaningful practice through play-based and explicit activities. In-the-moment feedback is something that Early Years practitioners do exceptionally well.

And let us not forget phonics. Direct instruction, an integral component of Rosenshine's Principles, has long been utilised in Early Years education, particularly in the teaching of phonics. Daily phonics lessons provide an excellent example of how Rosenshine's Principles can be incorporated into teaching practices for young children. When implemented thoughtfully and adapted to suit the unique needs of the class, direct instruction can significantly benefit Early Learners.

In the context of phonics lessons, several of Rosenshine's Principles can be observed.

Daily review Phonics lessons typically begin with a review of previously taught phonemes (the smallest units of sound) and graphemes (the written representation of these sounds). It helps young children solidify their knowledge and retain information more effectively.

Explicit instruction and modelling Teachers present new phonemes and graphemes through clear explanations and demonstrations, assisting pupils in understanding how to produce the sounds and form words correctly.

Guided practice Pupils engage in guided practice activities, where the teacher offers support and scaffolding, allowing children to practise their newly acquired phonics skills with guidance.

Independent practice Pupils are given opportunities to apply their phonics knowledge independently, reinforcing their learning through activities such as reading and writing.

Monitoring and feedback Teachers monitor pupil progress during phonics lessons, providing immediate and constructive feedback to help children improve their skills and understanding.

Case Study

Ms G. is a teacher who has been using play-based learning in her classroom for many years. She firmly believes that children learn best through play and she has seen first-hand how her class engage more fully in their learning when presented in a fun and engaging way. However, Ms G. also recognises the importance of explicit learning, especially when teaching vocabulary.

As she began incorporating Rosenshine's Principles of Instruction into her teaching practices, Ms G. found that she could balance play-based learning and explicit instruction. For example, at the beginning of each vocabulary lesson, Ms G. reviews the previous lesson's vocabulary words.

This review is done playfully, using games and activities reinforcing the children's prior learning. By doing so, she ensures that her pupils have a solid foundation for the new material she will present.

Next, Ms G. presents new vocabulary words in small steps, providing models of how to use the words in context. She engages the children in questioning and discussion, encouraging them to think about the words' meanings and how they might use them in their writing and speaking.

Ms G. then guides the pupils in practice activities in small groups and independently. She scaffolds the activities to ensure that each child is working at their own pace and level of understanding, providing support as needed. She gives feedback in the moment, providing praise and constructive criticism to help her class improve their skills and understanding.

Throughout the week, Ms G. incorporates the taught vocabulary words into various play-based activities. For example, she might set up a vocabulary scavenger hunt. Ms G. sets up a vocabulary scavenger hunt using pictures of the words instead of words. She hides the images around the classroom and sends her pupils on a search to find them. Once they find a picture, they have to say the word it represents out loud and give an example of how to use it in a sentence, or use vocabulary words as prompts for imaginative play. These activities allow the children to practise their new vocabulary in a playful, engaging way while reinforcing their learning.

At the end of the week, Ms G. engages the children to review the week's vocabulary words. She encourages them to use the words in sentences and discussions, helping them solidify their understanding and retention of the new material.

Ms G.'s approach to teaching vocabulary is a perfect example of how Rosenshine's Principles of Instruction can be adapted to suit the unique needs of young children. She provides a balance of play-based learning and explicit instruction, ensuring that her pupils are engaged and motivated while also learning the necessary skills and concepts. Her use of scaffolding and in-the-moment feedback allows her to meet the developmental needs of each child in her classroom, ensuring that they can all progress and succeed.

Drawing from the successful implementation of Rosenshine's Principles in phonics instruction, there is no reason why we cannot replicate this success in vocabulary acquisition lessons.

Top Tips

Chapter 5 discusses these tips more fully within the context of my GUIDE model.

Begin each lesson with a short review of previously learned vocabulary words, using flashcard images to prompt pupils' memory.

Introduce new vocabulary words incrementally – ideally 1–2 new words per lesson. Use visuals and real-life objects to provide context and meaning for the new words.

Give pupils time to practise using new vocabulary words in sentences orally. You can facilitate this by putting the children in pairs or small groups. Offer support and guidance as needed, and provide immediate feedback to help them refine their usage.

Use games and activities to engage pupils in the active practice of new vocabulary. For example, play 'I Spy' or a matching game, where pupils must connect the word to its correct image or simple definition.

Model the correct pronunciation and usage of new vocabulary words by incorporating them into classroom conversations and stories teachers read. Encourage pupils to listen for the new words and praise them when they use the words correctly in context.

Create a word wall or vocabulary chart in the classroom, displaying new words along with their images. Encourage pupils to use the word wall during independent practice and writing activities.

Engage pupils to regularly review vocabulary words by incorporating them into daily routines and songs.

In response to those who argue that Rosenshine's Principles focus too much on teacher-directed instruction, I assert that a balance can be achieved and I have certainly managed this in my classroom. As teachers, we can incorporate these principles into a child-centred and play-based approach alongside times of direct instruction, all promoting exploration and structure. It allows us to attend to the developmental needs of young children while providing a solid foundation for future learning. I have found that using these techniques leads to higher engagement, understanding and independent usage from my pupils.

KEY TAKEAWAYS

- Rosenshine's Principles of Instruction can be adapted for Early Years education, supporting young learners' cognitive, social and emotional development.
- Fundamental principles such as review, questioning, modelling, practice and monitoring can be integrated into Early Years teaching practices.
- Phonics instruction is a successful example of applying Rosenshine's Principles in Early Years education.
- A balance between child-centred, play-based approaches and direct instruction can provide a strong foundation for future learning.

> **Pause for Reflection**
>
> Considering your educational setting, how will you adapt and apply Rosenshine's Principles of Instruction to support your pupils' learning? What immediate changes can you make?

COGNITIVE LOAD THEORY

Cognitive Load Theory (CLT) emphasises the importance of managing the demands on a learner's working memory during the learning process. Our working memory has limited capacity and, when it becomes overloaded, it can impede learning and understanding (Sweller, 1988). As teachers, we must be mindful of the cognitive load we place on our young learners and design our instruction accordingly to optimise learning.

I was guilty of it when I started teaching. I often created overly complicated PowerPoint presentations that I thought must be absolutely wonderful for the children because they were full of colours and characters and things whizzing across the screen. What I was actually doing was overloading my poor little kiddo's brains. How on earth could they focus on what I was attempting to teach them when three giant cartoon bumble bees were flying on the screen?

Not only that, often my instructions would include multiple directions at once, meaning that once I got to the end of my speech, the children had forgotten the first thing I had said. I wish I had access to this information when I first started teaching!

Now, let us consider Rosenshine's Principles. These ten research-based instructional strategies, as we have discussed earlier, provide a framework for effective teaching that promotes pupil success. But how do these principles connect to Cognitive Load Theory? The answer lies in the fact that Rosenshine's Principles inherently account for the limitations of working memory and help us manage the cognitive load that our pupils experience. Here are a few examples.

Daily review By reviewing prior knowledge, we help pupils strengthen their long-term memory, making it easier to access and build upon this information without overburdening their working memory (Rosenshine, 2012).

Scaffolding and modelling When we break complex tasks into smaller, manageable steps and model how to perform them, we reduce the cognitive load on our pupils, making it easier for them to grasp and apply new concepts (Van Merriënboer and Sweller, 2005).

Guided practice Providing guidance and support as pupils practise new skills allows us to manage the cognitive demands placed on them, ensuring that they are challenged without becoming overwhelmed (Kirschner et al., 2006)

It is clear that when we apply Rosenshine's Principles in our classrooms, we are not only following evidence-based best practices, but also managing the cognitive load experienced by our pupils. As teachers, we are responsible for ensuring that our instruction is tailored to our pupils' needs, allowing them to learn effectively and confidently.

KEY TAKEAWAYS

- Cognitive Load Theory highlights the importance of managing demands on learners' working memory to optimise learning.
- Rosenshine's Principles inherently account for working memory limitations and help manage cognitive load.
- Fundamental principles, such as daily review, scaffolding and guided practice, support effective learning by reducing cognitive load.

Pause for Reflection

Considering your current teaching practices, how are you currently managing the cognitive load for your young learners, and what changes might you make to better address the cognitive demands in your educational setting?

Case Study

Meet Ms K., a dedicated and passionate Reception teacher who has taught for over seven years. She recognises the importance of vocabulary development in her young learners. She uses Cognitive Load Theory (Sweller, 1988) and Rosenshine's Principles of Instruction (Rosenshine, 2012) to guide her planning and delivery of vocabulary lessons.

At the beginning of the term, Ms K. set the stage for success by carefully selecting a list of essential vocabulary words that her pupils would be learning. She was mindful of their developmental stage and chose words that would be meaningful and relevant to their lives and experiences.

To minimise cognitive load, Ms K. grouped the vocabulary words into smaller, more manageable sets, gradually introducing them to her pupils over several weeks. Each day, she used Rosenshine's Principle of the daily review to reinforce previously taught words before introducing new ones, ensuring that her pupils had a strong foundation before moving on.

Ms K. found creative ways to present new vocabulary words clearly and concisely, using visuals, real-life objects and gestures to support her explanations. She followed Rosenshine's advice on clear instruction and modelling by demonstrating the correct usage of the words in sentences, encouraging her pupils to mimic her usage in various contexts.

To provide ample opportunities for practice, Ms K. designed a range of engaging activities that promoted both guided and independent practice. For instance, during circle time, she led the class in a 'word-of-the-day' activity where pupils took turns using the target vocabulary word in a sentence. Then, during centre time, the pupils participated in different vocabulary games that required them to apply their newly acquired words in a fun and interactive manner.

Throughout the day, Ms K. remained vigilant, monitoring her pupils' progress and offering timely feedback to support their vocabulary development. She frequently adjusted her teaching based on her observations, scaffolding and tailoring her instruction to cater to the diverse needs of her pupils.

By the end of the term, it was evident that Ms K.'s strategic and deliberate approach to vocabulary instruction, grounded in Cognitive Load Theory and Rosenshine's Principles, had paid off. Her pupils demonstrated impressive growth in their vocabulary knowledge and, more importantly, they were confident and eager to express themselves using their newly acquired words.

> Ms K.'s case study is an inspiring example of how a thoughtful and informed approach to vocabulary instruction can make a significant difference in the lives of young learners. By integrating Cognitive Load Theory and Rosenshine's Principles into her daily practice, Ms K. has successfully created a nurturing and engaging learning environment that supports her pupils' language development and paves the way for future academic success.

SUMMING UP

There is immense value in applying these theories and principles judiciously in our classrooms.

I hope to have demonstrated the importance of being mindful of our pupils' cognitive load (Sweller, 1988) as we equip them with the necessary tools for future language development success.

By embracing Rosenshine's Principles (2012), recognising the need to break down complex tasks, providing clear models and scaffolding, and offering ample opportunities for practice and feedback, we create the best possible supportive learning environment for our little learners.

In addition to the immense value these theories and principles bring to classrooms, understanding and applying them have significantly enhanced my teaching practice. They have equipped me with a profound insight into the mechanisms of learning and cognition, enabling me to curate teaching strategies that are not only effective but also cognisant of the unique needs of my students.

By breaking down complex information into digestible parts, you can better manage the cognitive load placed on children. The principles laid out by Rosenshine will also support scaffolding learning, modelling tasks and providing feedback. By implementing these principles, you should see notable improvements in your pupils' understanding and mastery of new concepts. Regular practice, coupled with timely and constructive feedback, will help develop a classroom environment conducive to learning. This approach ensures that learning becomes an engaging, rather than overwhelming, process for them.

Not only have these theories and principles improved my teaching practice, but they have also tangibly benefitted the classes I have taught. I have witnessed learning flourish, confidence grow, and children's passion for knowledge deepen. By embracing these theories and principles in my practice, I have provided my pupils with the best possible tools for success, shaping a generation of capable, confident and curious learners. These theories, backed by my personal experience, shape my teaching ethos: that every child, given the right support, can thrive and reach their true potential.

> **Pause for Reflection**
>
> How can you utilise the concepts of Cognitive Load Theory and Rosenshine's instructional Principles to build a nurturing learning environment for your children?

ACTION PLAN

Table 3.2 Top Tips for Practitioners Implementing Rosenshine's Principles in Vocabulary Acquisition Lessons

Action	Currently in Place	Next Steps
Provide regular assessments to monitor progress and identify areas that need further attention. Use the data collected to adjust the teaching methods and curriculum to better meet each child's needs.		
Review Rosenshine's Principles of Instruction and become familiar with the strategies outlined in the principles.		
Familiarise yourself with Cognitive Load Theory (CLT) and the limits of working memory.		
Identify areas in the curriculum where Rosenshine's Principles can be adapted and integrated thoughtfully into Early Years education without sacrificing developmental needs.		
Conduct a baseline assessment to identify the key vocabulary words that pupils need to learn based on their developmental stage and relevance to their lives and experiences.		
Monitor progress and provide feedback. Remain vigilant throughout the day, monitoring learners' progress and offering timely feedback to support their vocabulary development.		

4
WHICH WORDS?

When embarking on the voyage of vocabulary acquisition for Reception-aged children, it becomes clear that one of the fundamental challenges we face as educators is deciding 'which words?' to teach. This chapter will guide you through carefully selecting the most fitting words for your class. I will discuss the criteria for selection, how to cater to different vocabulary levels and the impact of context on vocabulary acquisition.

To provide a rich and meaningful learning environment for pupils, we must grapple with the sometimes daunting task of selecting the most appropriate and beneficial vocabulary that caters to learners' unique needs, backgrounds and experiences.

The initial focus will be on identifying the optimal vocabulary to unveil. We will expand on vocabulary tiers, as outlined by notable linguists Beck, McKeown and Kucan (2013), adapting their three-tier classification to fit the unique requirements of our Reception Year learners. I will break down the language learning journey into three levels and guide you in pitching your teaching at each stage.

We will consider how to select topic-specific vocabulary, ensuring that pupils are equipped with the necessary language tools to engage and fully understand the subjects at hand.

Additionally, we will explore how to optimise using storybooks for vocabulary teaching. We will analyse how these narratives, rich in varied language, can be harnessed effectively to broaden our pupils' word banks.

Selecting and planning for concept words will be discussed separately in Chapter 6.

I want to empower you with the skills to select the 'right' words for your class. Instead of finding the process longwinded and overwhelming, I aim to transform it into an enriching, insightful process that has the potential to significantly enhance your pupils' vocabulary acquisition journey.

SELECTING VOCABULARY TO 'UNVEIL'

Identifying the optimal vocabulary to introduce to children is an essential starting point in any teaching endeavour. The vocabulary should be unfamiliar to most children yet frequent enough to reappear naturally in their learning journey. By selecting apt words, we create an environment where children can naturally reinforce and deepen their understanding over time without needing significant additional planning time from the teacher.

Think of it as a Goldilocks challenge of finding words that are 'just right' – not too simplistic, not overly complex, but ideally suited to the learning needs of your pupils (Stahl and Nagy, 2005). Over time, this selection process becomes almost second nature with practice. It is crucial to dedicate sufficient time and thought to this task, as it could have a far-reaching impact on your learners' vocabulary development. This book has no prescribed list of words that children should know at a specific age; it varies significantly based on their experiences and surroundings.

Context dramatically influenced the vocabulary of the children I taught. In the heart of inner-city London, the pupils were exposed to language that reflected the city around them. When I began teaching them, an initial assessment showed me that most knew the word 'river' because of the River Thames, yet the majority had no idea what a 'cliff' was.

However, when I moved to teach in a small, deprived coastal town, the children's vocabulary painted a very different picture, resonating with their unique life experiences by the sea. Barely any children in the class knew the word 'city' or that 'London' was the capital city. Their vocabulary reflected their surroundings.

KEY TAKEAWAYS

- Identifying suitable vocabulary to introduce to children is critical to their learning journey. The selected words should be new to most learners yet frequent enough to recur naturally.
- The context in which children grow up can significantly influence their vocabulary. Children's language skills often mirror their experiences and surroundings.

Pause for Reflection

How does the environment and community surrounding your school shape your students' vocabulary and language experiences? How can you balance the need to expand their linguistic horizons while building upon their existing knowledge and experiences when selecting words to introduce?

VOCABULARY LEVELS

Early targeting of key vocabulary should be built into the curriculum from the beginning of Reception. Ensuring that a child truly understands a word, rather than merely repeating it, is crucial for them to acquire it as part of their vocabulary (Nation, 2001). As Chapter 1 mentions, ask yourself if a child's development will be hindered without knowledge of a particular word. If the answer is yes, then it is time to teach them the word.

According to Beck et al. (2013), words can be classified into three tiers, as shown in the table below.

Table 4.1 Beck et al.'s Vocabulary Tiers (2013)

Tier One	Basic words (e.g., dog, happy, jump). These words are often used and understood without much effort.
Tier Two	High-frequency words that can be found across various domains (e.g., analyse, summarise, illustrate). These words are necessary for understanding more complex ideas and require explicit instruction.
Tier Three	Low-frequency, domain-specific words (e.g., photosynthesis, metamorphosis, isosceles). These words are typically taught in relation to specific subject areas.

Although Tier One words are typically seen as being used and understood without much effort, we must ensure that we get children to a place where this is happening. We know that our little learners are still learning those biologically primary skills, and part of that learning is basic vocabulary. Building a strong foundation in basic words is crucial for supporting the later acquisition of Tier Two and Tier Three words.

Tier One words form the building blocks of language comprehension. These words are the most frequently used in daily conversations and are essential for children to grasp the meaning of sentences and express their thoughts effectively (Nation, 2001). Research shows that a child's Tier One vocabulary size strongly predicts overall language and reading development (Cunningham and Stanovich, 1997).

We already know that Cognitive Load Theory is about finding that sweet spot when introducing new information to our pupils, ensuring that their brains are challenged but not overwhelmed (Sweller, 1988). When we focus on building a strong foundation in Tier One words, we essentially give our young learners the tools they need to handle the mental effort required for learning more complex vocabulary later on.

With all of that being considered, we are looking at a slightly different, age-specific classification tailored for the language acquisition of 4–6-year olds. Table 4.2 shows how the levels have been broken down.

Table 4.2 Vocabulary Acquisition Word Levels for 4–6-year-olds

Level One	This is the primary level, which contains essential, everyday words. These are primarily concrete nouns, basic verbs and simple adjectives. Historically, we have assumed that most children acquire these naturally through interactions at home and in their surroundings. Words such as 'dog', 'milk', 'run' and 'happiness' fall under this category.
	Although these words can be picked up without formal instruction, it is crucial to remember that not all children have the same exposure or linguistic environment.
	Consequently, we still dedicate a portion of our explicit teaching to these words, ensuring that all pupils have a solid foundation to build their vocabulary.
Level Two	These words are more complex and descriptive, but still high-frequency words that children should ideally know or be learning by the time they exit Reception. They are commonly found in picture books, but may only be used occasionally in conversation at home.
	Examples might include words like 'excited', 'whisper', 'gallop', etc. These words often require explicit instruction and repeated exposure within the learning environment to understand fully.
Level Three	These words are low-frequency and specific to particular contexts or topics but enrich a child's language. These words often emerge from thematic learning or content areas in the curriculum. These require explicit teaching and tend to be learned in context. Words like 'construction', etc., might be at this level.

As underscored already, numerous children begin their journey in Reception facing a significant vocabulary deficit. In the context of the GUIDE framework detailed in Chapter 5, many of these pupils will need help with Level One words, the rudimentary building blocks of their linguistic development. These words allow children to convey their basic needs, express simple thoughts and comprehend everyday interactions.

The goal, therefore, is to ensure that by the time our young learners leave Reception, they are thoroughly grounded in Level One words. We want them to possess a commanding grasp of these basic terms that enable them to navigate their day-to-day experiences successfully.

Beyond this, we want children to equip themselves with a rich repertoire of Level Two words by the end of their Reception year. This achievement would see them comfortably using more complex yet high-frequency words that elevate their ability to comprehend and articulate increasingly nuanced thoughts and ideas.

Remember that every child is unique; some children may be able to secure some usage of Level Three words. The Reception year aim should be to introduce Level Three words based on the children's experiences and learning themes.

This gradual, intentional vocabulary instruction will give children the language tools they need for literacy and academic success.

Despite the seeming simplicity of Level One words, we must recognise the necessity of explicit instruction even at this fundamental stage. As we have deliberated in previous chapters, the understanding and use of these words may not come naturally to all children, particularly those with a vocabulary deficit. Similarly, transitioning to Level Two and eventually Level Three words necessitates a deliberate and focused teaching approach. We, as educators, must weave explicit instruction into the rich tapestry of experiences we provide to ensure that no child is left behind in their vocabulary journey.

Drawing from my experience teaching in diverse settings, I have witnessed first-hand the marked difference in children's vocabulary exposure in their long-term memory. This divergence underscores the contextual importance of choosing vocabulary. The one-size-fits-all approach is futile. Instead, we, as teachers, must be responsive to our pupils' unique needs and experiences, making strategic word choices that most benefit their linguistic growth.

Understanding a child's unique context and background is pivotal in vocabulary selection. The variance in vocabulary exposure in different settings emphasises the need for a tailored approach. As educators, our strategic word choices should be based on our pupils' unique needs and experiences, ensuring maximum linguistic growth.

KEY TAKEAWAYS

- Level One vocabulary consists of everyday words that children should ideally acquire naturally through interactions. However, it is essential to remember that not all children have the same exposure or linguistic environment, and many children are still in the process of learning these words.
- Level Two vocabulary is more complex with high-frequency words.
- Level Three words are lower frequency and context-specific words that can enrich a child's language. Despite their low frequency, these words can significantly enhance a child's comprehension and expression when taught effectively.

Pause for Reflection

Reflect on your pupils' current vocabulary knowledge. How do you typically choose the vocabulary you teach, and does it account for the varying levels of language exposure among your pupils? Where do your pupils currently sit within the levels?

Case Study

Mr U., a dedicated teacher in a busy northern town, faces the challenge of selecting appropriate vocabulary for his Reception class's new topic, 'Where People Live'. Mr U. recognises that their experiences and surroundings influence pupils' vocabulary. Living in a busy northern town, the children's linguistic environment has shaped their existing vocabulary. However, it is crucial to note that not all children have the same exposure or opportunities to develop language skills. A careful assessment reveals that while some words like 'train' are familiar due to their local context, other words like 'rock pool' are entirely unfamiliar to most pupils.

To guide his vocabulary selection process, Mr U. uses the GUIDE level classifications for the language acquisition of 4–6-year-olds.

Reflecting on his pupils' language abilities, Mr U. realises that many face a significant vocabulary deficit. Some children struggle even with Level One words, the basic building blocks of their linguistic development. Mr U. understands that the key goal in the Reception year is for pupils to master Level One words, enabling them to express their basic needs, comprehend everyday interactions and lay the foundation for further language acquisition.

Mr U. recognises that dedicating explicit teaching time to Level One words will provide his pupils with the necessary language tools to navigate their day-to-day experiences successfully.

Mr U. carefully selects two weeks' worth of Level One words that align with the needs and experiences of his Reception class. He considers their unique context, ensuring that the chosen words are not too simplistic or overly complex. By introducing words that are 'just right', Mr U. creates an environment where children can naturally reinforce and deepen their understanding over time without significant additional planning on his part.

For the initial two-week period, Mr U. chooses Level One words that align with the class's first thematic learning topic of 'Where People Live'. He considers the children's immediate surroundings and wider context. The selected Level One words include:

- village
- town
- city
- roof
- street
- garden
- market
- farm
- pier
- field
- house
- flat
- tall
- short
- open
- close.

Mr U. observed that many of the children he taught lived in flats. Recognising the need to expand their understanding, he includes the words 'house' and 'flat' in his vocabulary selection. It becomes evident that some children were unaware that 'home' could encompass an entire house where someone could live independently. In contrast, other children who resided in houses were unfamiliar with living in a flat. By introducing these words, Mr U. aims to broaden the children's awareness and promote a comprehensive understanding of different living spaces within their community.

As the pupils become more proficient with Level One words, Mr U. gradually introduces Level Two words after the initial two-week period to enhance their vocabulary further. These words are more complex, offering higher language sophistication. Mr U. conducts focus groups with his teaching assistant to provide additional support and explicit teaching with Level One words for pupils requiring further support.

The selected Level Two words include:

- crowded
- spacious
- cosy
- community
- charming
- terrace
- cottage
- barn
- peaceful
- modern
- comfortable
- stroll
- explore
- decorate
- visit.

By addressing the vocabulary deficit and strategically introducing Level One words related to the thematic learning topic of 'Where People Live', Mr U. provides his pupils with a solid foundation for language development. He acknowledges the immediate surroundings of the children, as well as other living environments like villages and coastal areas, to ensure a comprehensive understanding of different types of homes and communities.

Additionally, as his pupils progress, Mr U. incorporates Tier Two words to expand their vocabulary and enable them to express more nuanced thoughts and ideas. Through focus groups and explicit teaching, Mr U. ensures that all pupils receive the necessary support to enhance their linguistic growth and academic success.

TOPIC WORDS

Throughout the Reception year, children delve into a variety of fascinating topics. However, the depth and richness of their understanding of these topics greatly depends on their grasp of the associated vocabulary. Children are less likely to grasp the whole teaching of a pirate's topic if they are unfamiliar with terms like 'sword', 'parrot' or 'treasure'.

The topic can fall short if our pupils lack the necessary word bank to comprehend and engage with the subject matter. Therefore, we must conscientiously teach topic-specific vocabulary, considering that many of these words could be applied to various contexts and themes, thus expanding the children's overall linguistic repertoire. Once children have a larger bank of vocabulary, they will be able to make those connections.

In my own experience as a teacher, leader and teaching coach, I have had the pleasure of observing various Early Years practitioners in action. Most are adept at identifying and explaining new words through images or brief descriptions, which is commendable. However, there is scope for enhancement. Consider this: what if those practitioners used a more structured approach to vocabulary instruction, predicated on careful planning and a systematic teaching sequence? What if they ensured that words make their way into the children's long-term memory, aiding their future comprehension and communication?

When venturing into a new topic, before the topic begins, think about the knowledge, skills and understanding you want your learners to know and have by the end of the topic. From there, plot out which words your learners need to understand to fully lay the foundations for that learning. While pre-existing schemes of work might suggest some vocabulary and are helpful, we must be cautious to ensure that we do not rely solely on them. Always consider your specific context and cohort.

When doing this, it is beneficial to think of a healthy selection of nouns, verbs and adjectives. Nouns are always the easiest to teach, but children must be exposed to a wide variety of language. Once you have done that, assess whether the words fall under Level One, Level Two or Level Three.

While doing this, also reflect on your knowledge of your cohorts' current vocabulary knowledge. In some topics, your class, for whatever reason specific to them, may already know the vast majority of Level One words that you have decided need to be known. It is also worth ensuring that you speak with your support staff and other teachers on your phase to help make your choices. When teaching in London, I found my students were already familiar with many Level One words related to public transport. Therefore, we could focus more on Levels Two and Three transport words in our city-related topics.

Remember time constraints – you can effectively teach only so many words in a given period. Therefore, your selection should be precise and considered, aimed at maximising coverage and acquisition. With careful planning, systematic instruction and a deep understanding of your learners, you can truly enrich their vocabulary and, consequently, their comprehension of the world around them.

EXAMPLE OF VOCABULARY PLANNING FOR FOOD TOPIC

Please note that these are examples only. All Early Years settings are unique, and what may be appropriate for some settings may not be for others.

Table 4.3 An Example of Vocabulary Planning for a Food Topic in Reception

	Nouns	Adjectives	Verbs
Level One	Vegetable	Yummy	Eat
	Fruit	Hot	Drink
	Milk	Cold	Chew
	Juice	Warm	Mix
	Bread	Soft	Bite
	Water	Crunchy	
	Plate		
	Cup		
	Oven		
	Pudding		
Level Two	Broccoli	Delicious	Gobble
	Saucepan	Salty	Nibble
	Cucumber	Ripe	Peel
	Omelette	Savoury	Mash
	Whisk	Frozen	Stir
		Juicy	Roast
		Tasty	Chop
Level Three	Pomegranate	Delectable	Drain
	Sieve	Succulent	Blend
	Fillet	Appetising	Ingest
	Crockery	Bitter	Digest

KEY TAKEAWAYS

- The depth and richness of children's understanding of various topics depend heavily on their grasp of the related vocabulary. We must intentionally teach topic-specific words to allow pupils to fully engage and understand the subject matter.
- The effectiveness of vocabulary teaching can be significantly enhanced with a systematic teaching approach, carefully planned and consistently applied to ensure that new words are embedded into children's long-term memory.
- When choosing vocabulary for a specific topic, it is crucial to consider the pre-existing knowledge of the class and the context they come from to tailor the instruction to cater to the cohort's needs.
- It is beneficial to include a healthy selection of nouns, verbs and adjectives in our vocabulary instruction. While nouns may be the easiest to teach, exposing children to a wide range of language types broadens their linguistic competence.

- Educators must strategically select the number and complexity of words to teach during a given period. The goal should be to maximise coverage and acquisition through precise selection and considered instruction.

> **Pause for Reflection**
>
> Reflect on a recent topic you have taught or plan to teach. Have you identified the critical vocabulary that children need to engage fully with this topic? How did you decide on these words, and did you consider the balance between nouns, verbs and adjectives? Does your chosen vocabulary reflect your pupils' specific needs and prior knowledge?

STORYBOOK WORDS

Storybooks serve as the heart and soul of a Reception classroom. They become magical portals for children to explore, comprehend and empathise with various life situations. These stories often claim a cherished spot in a child's daily routine. It is crucial that we ensure that every child can fully enjoy storytime, unhindered by gaps in their language comprehension.

During my first year of teaching, I had a profound learning experience centred around a Key Stage 1 child who displayed a peculiar pattern during storytime. Typically a spirited and involved learner, this little girl would become noticeably restless during our reading sessions. She would detach from the group and fidget incessantly, and her eyes would reflect a desire to be anywhere but listening to the story. Interestingly, this behaviour was far less prominent when reading familiar stories, the 'class classics', which puzzled me.

Following my instinct, I decided to speak to her. Initially, she hesitated to share her feelings, but I sensed her distress. After a moment of silence, I gently asked her, 'Do you understand the stories when I read them?' Her response was a sad shake of the head.

This encounter was a significant wake-up call. It highlighted the importance of ensuring that children understand the vocabulary they were exposed to. I generally made a conscious effort to explain new vocabulary in the rest of my lessons (albeit not in the structured way I do now). Still, when it came to storytime, I would often just read for enjoyment, bypassing the opportunity to explain unfamiliar words unless they were notably complex Level 3 terms. At that moment, when I was looking into my learner's eyes, I realised that in doing so, I was inadvertently doing the children I taught a massive disservice. They deserved a more comprehensive approach to vocabulary exposure, and from that point on, I promised to do just that.

Class storybooks can be an absolutely wonderful way to expose your class to unfamiliar vocabulary because they often contain language that is richer and more colourful than day-to-day conversation, making them a treasure trove for vocabulary expansion. However, what is important is to ensure that that vocabulary is understood. By deliberately teaching unfamiliar words drawn from storybooks, we not only enhance a child's comprehension and literacy development, but we also enrich their spoken language repertoire.

The pivotal factor here is astute selection. There may be the occasional word in the story that can very quickly be explained in the moment – terms specific to the story, unlikely to recur or relatively easy to grasp; other words require meticulous teaching. This underscores the importance of thoughtful book selection. A spontaneous choice of a storybook from the shelf for an impromptu reading session may not allow you the time to plan and conduct your mini vocabulary lesson effectively.

While this approach demands proactive planning and foresight, the outcomes are undoubtedly rewarding. Trust me, you will soon notice a swift growth in your class's vocabulary and an increased frequency of students using the taught words in conversation. The fruits of this labour are undoubtedly worth the investment.

Similar to the approach with topic-related words, it is vital to collaborate with colleagues and bear your class's unique needs in mind when choosing words from storybooks. Your aim should be to select words that deepen a child's story comprehension and broaden their spoken vocabulary.

In contrast to topic vocabulary, you may find yourself leaning towards more adjectives and verbs when selecting words from storybooks, given their narrative nature. Don't worry! It is perfectly acceptable. While it is essential to ensure that children have a firm grasp of Level One words, certain books may naturally encompass a greater quantity of Level Two words, which is acceptable. What is crucial is that your Level One words are robust and taught in other contexts and that the book aligns with your class's capability.

While we seek to introduce an appropriate level of challenge for the children, we must avoid choosing an excessively complex storybook. The goal is not to overwhelm the children with difficulty but to maintain comprehensibility, ensuring that their learning journey is stimulating and enjoyable.

Case Study

Mrs E., an experienced Reception teacher, is introducing her class to the joys of *The Gruffalo*, a beloved story for this age group. She recognises the rich vocabulary in the book and sees it as an excellent opportunity to expand her pupils' word knowledge.

As part of her preparations, Mrs E. selects key nouns, adjectives and verbs from the text that cater to various difficulty levels. She opts for words that are vital for understanding the story's plot and enriching the children's spoken language, considering her class's learning needs and abilities.

Among the chosen words, she includes some essential Level One vocabulary: 'stream' and 'roar', and Level Two adjectives and verbs such as 'terrible', 'roasted', 'poisonous', 'knobbly', 'deep' and 'astounding'.

Aware that her pupils need to understand these words before they dive into the story, Mrs E. arranges a pre-reading vocabulary session. In this mini lesson, she explains each word, creates associations, uses the words in different sentences and encourages the children to do the same.

For example, when teaching the word 'terrible', Mrs E. draws pictures of things that might be considered terrible, like a giant scary dinosaur or a thunderstorm. She presents these vivid mental images to the children and then encourages them to draw similar pictures on mini whiteboards.

When teaching the word 'stream', Mrs E. shows a video of a gently flowing stream, explaining that it is a small river, and emphasises its calmness. She also invites the children to mimic a stream's sound and imitate the movement with their hands, reinforcing the sensory associations.

Once she has thoroughly taught these words, Mrs E. and her class dive into The Gruffalo. As they read, Mrs E. points out and reinforces the taught vocabulary whenever these words appear in the text.

In the following vocabulary sessions unrelated to The Gruffalo, Mrs E. incorporates retrieval practice. She uses the taught words in new and varied contexts, asking questions such as 'What other things can be terrible?' or 'Can you think of a time when you might hear a roar?' to facilitate further usage and understanding of these new words.

Over time, she notices her pupils using words such as 'terrible' in their conversations and written work. It is a proud moment when one of them refers to a picture of a scary monster as having 'knobbly knees'.

This case study demonstrates how Mrs E. successfully used The Gruffalo not just as an entertaining storybook, but as a valuable tool for vocabulary acquisition. Mrs E.'s systematic approach, her careful selection of vocabulary and her use of retrieval practice serve as an effective strategy for introducing a new level of complexity in language, while keeping learning fun, engaging and accessible.

EXAMPLE OF VOCABULARY PLANNING FOR HALIBUT JACKSON

Please note that these are examples only. All Early Years settings are unique and what may be appropriate for some settings may not be for others.

Table 4.4 An Example of Vocabulary Planning for the *Halibut Jackson* Storybook

	Nouns	Adjectives	Verbs
Level One	Invitation		
Level Two	Background Suit Indoors	Grand	Glittering
Level Three			Longed

KEY TAKEAWAYS

- Storybooks in a Reception classroom are potent vehicles for language acquisition. Rich in diverse vocabulary, these books can expose children to words that may not be commonly used in everyday conversations.
- Thoughtful book and word selection are crucial to effective vocabulary teaching. Teachers should choose books and words that cater to their class's unique needs and capabilities, considering the balance of nouns, verbs and adjectives. They should also plan their reading sessions in advance to effectively incorporate vocabulary instruction.
- While introducing new vocabulary through storybooks, teachers should aim to provide an appropriate level of challenge without overwhelming the children. The selected book and the introduced vocabulary must align with the class's capability.

Pause for Reflection

What is your current storytime practice? How often do you intentionally teach new vocabulary from the storybooks you read with your students? How could you systematically incorporate vocabulary instruction into your reading sessions to deepen the comprehension and enrich the spoken language repertoire of your learners?

SUMMING UP

Vocabulary plays a pivotal role in children's comprehension and engagement with various topics and subjects throughout their learning journey, one that goes far beyond the Reception year. A child's understanding and knowledge of topic-specific vocabulary can significantly influence their learning experience, encouraging a deeper and more enriched engagement with the subjects.

At the heart of this learning journey is the teacher. Teachers are the ones who interact with the children daily. You have an intimate understanding of your pupils' learning. You can gauge the complexity of vocabulary a child is ready to handle and can present the new words in a way that is most likely to resonate with them. In essence, teachers serve as the bridge between the world of new vocabulary and the children, using professional judgement and unique insights about the children to facilitate effective and enjoyable learning.

Moreover, teachers are often the first to witness the children's triumphs and challenges. You observe when a child uses a new word correctly in a conversation or struggles to remember a word they had previously learnt. These 'in-the-moment' assessments that teachers are known for, particularly in EYFS, provide real-time feedback, enabling teachers to adapt vocabulary instruction to suit the children's needs and progress. This is why having a good understanding, planning and delivery of vocabulary is vital.

The teacher plays a pivotal role in vocabulary instruction in the EYFS. Knowledge of the children, ability to assess their learning in real-time, and capacity to foster a positive learning environment collectively contribute to the children's vocabulary development.

I hope I have armed you with the tools and understanding necessary to navigate the challenge of vocabulary selection and instruction effectively. As an educator, you can illuminate the world of words for your pupils and pave their path towards rich linguistic understanding. This journey of vocabulary teaching is filled with immense possibilities and rewards.

With this knowledge and insight, you are well equipped to truly make a difference in your pupils' language-learning journey. Through thoughtful planning, intentional teaching and supportive encouragement, teachers can profoundly enrich their pupils' vocabulary, paving the way for their future learning and communication success.

Pause for Reflection

How can the insights gained from this chapter help you further refine your approach to vocabulary selection, planning and teaching, to enhance your pupils' language learning journey?

WHICH WORDS?

ACTION PLAN

Table 4.5 An Action Plan for Practitioners to Assess their Current Practice and Consider their Next Steps in Order to Successfully Implement Chapter 4's Actions

Action	Currently in Place	Next Steps
Use initial assessment data (referenced in Chapter 4's action plan) to gauge the vocabulary levels of your pupils. This helps identify their familiarity with Level One words and assess the extent of potential vocabulary deficit.		
Plan to reinforce Level One words through explicit teaching. Gradually introduce Level Two words and ensure that they are used in class activities, conversations and books read in class. Introduce key Level Three words, ideally connected to the curriculum's thematic learning or content areas.		
Regularly review pupils' vocabulary development and adjust your plan if necessary. Implement a weekly or monthly review system to monitor their progress and adjust teaching plans based on this feedback.		
Conduct a baseline assessment to identify the key vocabulary words that pupils need to learn based on their developmental stage and relevance to their lives and experiences.		
Monitor progress and provide feedback. Remain vigilant throughout the day, monitoring learners' progress and offering timely feedback to support their vocabulary development.		
Before a new topic begins, identify the vocabulary that will be necessary for the children to comprehend and engage with the subject matter fully. Consider your specific context and cohort in this selection. List the key vocabulary for each new topic, including a mix of nouns, verbs and adjectives.		
Decide on the books that you want to teach vocabulary from and create a long-term plan across the year, with the specific words you will focus on each week or month. Include a mix of nouns, verbs and adjectives. Note: there will naturally be more verbs and adjectives.		
Plan Vocabulary Teaching Sequence. With the vocabulary selected and classified, create a structured and systematic teaching sequence for the new topic. Develop a week-by-week teaching sequence for the topic vocabulary, with specific words targeted in each period.		
Once the vocabulary for storybooks/topics is identified, categorise the words into Level One, Level Two or Level Three, reflecting on your knowledge of the class's current vocabulary abilities. Classify the listed vocabulary into the appropriate levels, noting any words that most of the class already knows.		

5
THE GUIDE FRAMEWORK: HOW DO I PLAN A LESSON?

Building upon the foundation set in the previous chapter, this chapter will extend the discussion into the practicalities of teaching vocabulary, specifically emphasising my personal approach to explicit instruction with the GUIDE framework. This methodology is firmly grounded in the theoretical underpinnings of Rosenshine's Principles (Rosenshine, 2012) and Cognitive Load Theory (Sweller, 1988).

In my years as an educator, I have come to value the synergy between theory and practice. The abstract principles that guide our understanding of learning processes and cognitive function are not merely academic constructs; they are vital tools that can shape our pedagogical practices in the classroom. The interplay between these theories and real-life teaching is at the heart of this chapter, offering a detailed exploration of how theory can shape and inform teaching practice and vice versa.

Rosenshine's Principles, as discussed in Chapter 3, provide research-informed guidelines for effective teaching. In conjunction with an understanding of Cognitive Load Theory, these principles are central to my approach to direct instruction in vocabulary development. As we progress through this chapter, I will walk you through my process of vocabulary instruction step by step, elucidating how these principles manifest in the practical context of a real-world classroom.

Each component of the direct teaching process will be considered through the lens of Rosenshine's Principles and Cognitive Load Theory. With each step, I will offer practical tips and recommendations that have proven successful in my experience, while always tying back to our theoretical foundation.

I aim to illustrate how theory and practice can form a robust, adaptable approach to vocabulary instruction in Early Years education.

GUIDE

As introduced in Chapter 1, the GUIDE model is a systematic and clear framework I have developed to explicitly teach vocabulary in Reception and Key Stage 1. It is crafted to assist educators in providing the necessary guidance and support, ensuring that all students can thrive in their language development. The framework encapsulates the essential aspects of vocabulary teaching, serving as a streamlined guide for Early Years educators.

Table 5.1 The GUIDE Model: A Teaching Framework I have Developed to Explicitly Teach Vocabulary in Reception and Key Stage 1

Gather	Review and consolidate previously learned vocabulary words. • Use flashcards with vocabulary words and associated images. • Engage in quick games that require pupils to recall and use these words in sentences. • Utilise a 'Word of the Day' chart to revisit the previous day's vocabulary, discussing its meaning and context.
Unveil	Introduce selected new vocabulary words incrementally. • Accompany the unveiling of new words with visuals, real-life objects, or actions that provide context and meaning. • Model the use of the word in a variety of contexts. • Use 'My Turn, Your Turn' (you say, pupils repeat) so children can orally rehearse. • Connect new vocabulary words with pupils' prior experiences to create meaningful associations.
Interact	Facilitate oral practice of new vocabulary words. • Offer sentence frames or starters to scaffold pupils' verbal practice. • Encourage peer practice and provide immediate feedback. • Use games and activities to engage pupils in active vocabulary practice.
Demonstrate	Model correct usage and pronunciation of vocabulary words. • Highlight new vocabulary words during story time in classroom conversations and during wider learning. • Set up a recognition system for pupils who correctly use new words in context. • Use a word wall or vocabulary chart in the classroom to display new words and their images.
Embed	Incorporate regular review of vocabulary words into daily routines. • Assess pupils' vocabulary retention informally. • Use songs or rhymes to reinforce both new and previously learned vocabulary words. • Encourage pupils to 'teach' new words to each other or their families at home, creating a further layer of review and repetition.

The next section of this chapter will discuss in detail the first three parts of the GUIDE system – Gather, Unveil and Interact – which will form the basis of your daily vocabulary lesson. The two final sections – 'Demonstrate' and 'Embed' – will be detailed in Chapters 7 and 8.

GATHER

The 'Gather' stage of our GUIDE model encourages us to look back before we move forward. As paradoxical as it may sound, we employ an end-to-begin strategy. In this phase, we utilise previously taught words as part of a daily 'retrieval' practice. It is a core tenet of Rosenshine's principles – review and retrieval are essential for embedding new learning into long-term memory.

Here, we summon words from past lessons, allowing students to delve into their memory, retrieve the words and strengthen their cognitive recall. However, selecting the words for this retrieval practice requires careful consideration.

Research by Soderman et al. (2008) calls this 'spaced retrieval practice', suggesting that learning is significantly enhanced when reviews are spaced out and retrieval is more challenging, improving learners' retention and recall of those words. Weinstein and Sumeracki (2018) provide a comprehensive overview of the learning process, highlighting the importance of spaced retrieval.

In the Gather stage of our GUIDE model, we apply these principles, selecting words from various intervals to strengthen the robustness of memory recall, reflecting Weinstein and Sumeracki's emphasis on spaced practice as a tool for effective, long-term learning.

A balanced mixture of words should be employed to optimise the benefits of the Gather stage. You are both revisiting the words taught the previous day and introducing strategic spacing in your selection. In other words, you want a mixture of 'new–old' words.

Aim to have six gathered words. Two of them are fresh, taught the day before, and two others from the last week, still relatively new but only partially fresh. The final two words should be older ones introduced several weeks ago. This intentional spread across temporal intervals – a pedagogical application of the 'spacing effect' – has been found to strengthen the durability of memory recall (Cepeda et al., 2008).

Ensuring this variety, however, necessitates good organisation. A clear system of word organisation is crucial to keep track of when words were last reviewed and ensure comprehensive vocabulary coverage. This method enriches the pool of words that learners can retrieve and nurtures an environment where long-term memory is continuously reinforced.

The first part of the Gather portion of the lesson should always utilise flashcards. Each card should feature a vocabulary word on one side and an associated image on the other. The visual aids offer a tangible cue to support memory recall, anchoring the word to a concrete image in the learners' minds. Although these flashcards must be made, this need not be a timely affair. Making two a day for vocabulary sessions takes me 3 minutes at maximum. The flashcards then serve a dual function: they are used to present your two new words – in the next part of the lesson and repeatedly reused in different sessions to review vocabulary words in the Gather section. Before long, you end up with a massive bank of flashcards.

Engaging students in games like 'Word Relay' can transform vocabulary review into an enjoyable and communal experience, further enhancing retention (Zadina, 2014). In 'Word Relay', students form teams, and each team is given a set of vocabulary words. When the relay begins, the first student in each team comes up with a sentence using one of the given words, then passes the 'baton' (in this case, the word set) to the next team member, who does the same with a new word.

The cycle continues until all team members have had a turn and all the vocabulary words have been used in sentences. Such a game not only encourages recall, but also fosters a spirit of team collaboration, making learning more social and interactive.

A 'Word of the Day' chart can be a powerful Gather tool. This chart should feature the vocabulary word from the previous day's lesson. At the start of each new session, revisit this word, discussing its meaning, usage and context. Utilise this for a word that you want to place a particular focus on.

Example Gather Script

Teacher: Good morning, everyone! Today, we will start our day with a fun memory challenge. I have some flashcards here from our previous lessons.

[Teacher shows the first flashcard to the whole class.]

Teacher: Let's look at this word together. Tell your partner what it is. Yes, that's correct. It's '____'. Now, turn to your partner. Partner 1, explain what '____' means. Partner 2, use it in a sentence.'

[Children turn to their partners. Teacher circulates the room, listening to the pairs providing feedback.]

[Repeat the process for six Gather words.]

Teacher: Fantastic work, everyone! Now, let's play a quick game. It's called 'Word Detective'. I will describe something using words we've learned and you will try to guess what it is with your partner.

[Teacher provides a short, descriptive clue based on one of the previously learned vocabulary words.]

Teacher: For example, it is a small, colourful creature that can fly. Can anyone guess what it is?

[The game continues for 1–2 minutes, with the teacher providing more clues for different words.]

> Teacher: Great job, detectives! To wrap up the Gather stage, let's revisit our 'Word of the Day' from yesterday.
>
> [Teacher points to the 'Word of the Day' chart.]
>
> Teacher: Yesterday, we learned the word '____'. Partner 2, remind your partner what '____' means. Partner 1, can you use '___' in a sentence?
>
> [Children turn to their partners. Teacher circulates the room, listening to the pairs, providing feedback.]
>
> Teacher: Well done! I am impressed with your memory skills.

KEY TAKEAWAYS

- The Gather stage of the GUIDE model incorporates the principle of review and retrieval, a fundamental tenet of Rosenshine's Principles, to help embed new learning into long-term memory. It involves revisiting vocabulary words from previous lessons, stimulating memory retrieval and strengthening cognitive recall.
- Spaced retrieval practice, as suggested by Soderman et al. (2008), forms an integral part of the Gather stage, where words from various time intervals are reviewed, improving students' retention and recall.
- The Gather stage emphasises the need for a strategic mix of 'new–old' words and a well-organised word-tracking system to ensure comprehensive vocabulary coverage.
- Flashcards, games like 'Word Relay' and a 'Word of the Day' chart are practical tools in this stage. They make vocabulary review more engaging, enhance memory recall and offer opportunities for learners to use the words in context.

> **Pause for Reflection**
>
> Reflect on your current approach to vocabulary teaching. How might the strategies outlined in the Gather stage, such as using spaced retrieval practice and a variety of review activities, enhance your students' vocabulary recall and retention?

UNVEIL

Building on the groundwork in Chapter 4, where we delved into the art and science of selecting the most appropriate words for your lessons, we now transition to the next phase of the GUIDE model – 'Unveil'. This stage forms the crux of your lesson, the moment new words are introduced, or 'unveiled', to the little minds in your classroom.

Limiting the number of new words introduced in a single lesson is prudent. Overloading students with an excess of new vocabulary can lead to cognitive overload, a concept we explored in our discussion of Cognitive Load Theory in Chapter 3. To avoid this, I typically introduce two new words per lesson. However, this is not a hard-and-fast rule.

Sometimes, I introduce only one word, mainly if a complex term requires in-depth exploration. Conversely, there may be occasions when I introduce three words, especially if I believe the words will be more accessible to my students; this could be due to their prior knowledge that the new words can be linked to, or because of a contextual understanding that makes them more relatable.

Let's consider an example to illustrate this point. Suppose the vocabulary being taught relates to the seaside. The children in your class may already be familiar with words such as 'beach', 'sand' and 'sea'. In this context, introducing words such as 'coast', 'tide' and 'sandy' might be less daunting for them.

These new words can 'hang on' to their existing knowledge, bridging the familiar and the new. This approach not only makes the learning process more manageable, but also fosters a deeper understanding of the interconnectedness of language.

As we delve deeper into the Unveil stage of the GUIDE model, we will explore a series of strategies designed to introduce new words in as practical, engaging and snappy a manner as possible. Remember, we want the words to be remembered and understood, but we also want the learning to be fun. It is Early Years, after all! The whole process should take 3-4 minutes at maximum.

The first strategy involves using visuals, real-life objects, or actions to accompany the unveiling of new words; a powerful way to provide context and meaning for the new vocabulary. For example, suppose the new word is 'caterpillar'. In that case, you might show a picture of a caterpillar, bring in a toy caterpillar, or even act out the wriggly movement of a caterpillar.

This approach aligns with the Dual Coding Theory, which posits that information is more likely to be remembered if it is presented in both verbal and visual forms (Caviglioli, 2019). By associating the new word with a tangible object or action, you create a multisensory learning experience that can enhance memory and understanding. It also supports children with English as an additional language (EAL) and children who require speech and language support.

There may be instances where a word does not immediately lend itself to a pictorial representation. In such cases, engaging one of the other senses is beneficial to help convey the word's meaning. This multisensory approach can provide a more tangible understanding of the word and create a memorable learning experience that reinforces the word's meaning.

For example, a picture may not fully capture its meaning if you teach the word 'scrumptious'. Instead, you could provide the children with a 'scrumptious' experience, such as tasting delicious chocolate (with parental permission, of course). This sensory experience can help to solidify the meaning of 'scrumptious' in a way that a picture might not.

As the children taste the chocolate, you can reinforce the word's meaning by saying, 'This chocolate is scrumptious, isn't it?' A context has been provided for the word, creating a direct association between the word 'scrumptious' and the delightful experience of tasting chocolate.

Next, we model the use of the word in various contexts, which involves using the new word in different sentences and situations, showing students how the word can be used in real-life scenarios. For instance, if the new word is 'enormous', you might say, 'The elephant is enormous', 'I saw an enormous tree in the park', or 'My appetite is enormous after a long day at school'. Demonstrating the word's versatility, you are helping students understand its meaning more deeply and encouraging them to use it in their conversations.

Ensuring consistency across all practitioners within the year group is a critical aspect of effective vocabulary instruction. Children greatly benefit from a unified approach to vocabulary acquisition at this developmental stage. All adults involved in their education should have a shared understanding of the vocabulary being taught.

When a new word is introduced, all practitioners must know the specific definition taught to the children. This shared understanding allows for the consistent use of the word and its definition across different contexts, reinforcing the children's learning. Whether the word arises in the lesson or casual conversation beyond the classroom, the consistent use of the defined meaning helps to solidify the children's understanding and recall of the new vocabulary.

The 'My Turn, Your Turn' strategy is another effective tool for vocabulary instruction. In this approach, you say the new word and then the pupils repeat it. I used this in every area of my teaching in Reception. It was one of the top tools in my teaching toolkit. It allows children to orally rehearse the word, improving their pronunciation and helping them to remember it. It is a simple yet powerful technique that fosters active engagement and immediate feedback, critical elements of effective instruction.

Incorporating phonology into the 'Unveil' process is crucial in reinforcing the word's speech sounds, which is particularly important for children in the early years of development. As they are still developing their phonological awareness, engaging in activities highlighting words' phonetic components can significantly enhance their understanding and retention of new vocabulary.

One effective way to incorporate this is through syllable clapping. After introducing the new word and having the pupils repeat it in the 'My Turn, Your Turn' activity, invite the children to clap out the word's syllables. This activity helps children break down the word into phonetic components and provides a tactile and auditory experience that further reinforces their understanding.

For example, if the new word is 'elephant', you would clap three times – once for each syllable: 'el', 'e', 'phant'. This multisensory approach to phonology helps children connect the physical act of clapping with the auditory experience of hearing the syllables, thereby deepening their understanding of the word's structure and pronunciation.

Connecting new vocabulary words with pupils' prior experiences is another strategy that can enhance vocabulary acquisition. It involves linking the new word to something the students already know or have experienced. For example, if the new word is 'scorching', you might remind the students of a particularly hot summer day they experienced. By creating this link, you are helping students form meaningful associations that can aid in their understanding and retention of the new word.

Each of these strategies, when used effectively, can make the Unveil stage of the GUIDE model a powerful tool for vocabulary instruction. As with the Gather stage, the key is to be intentional and strategic in your approach, always considering the principles of effective instruction and cognitive load management. Doing so ensures that your vocabulary instruction is engaging and enjoyable for your students and deeply impactful in their language development.

Example Unveil Script

Teacher: Now that we've warmed up our brains with some words we already know, it's time to add some new ones to our vocabulary collection. Today, we are going to learn two new words. Are you ready?

[Teacher reveals the first flashcard with the new word and a corresponding image or object.]

Teacher: Our first new word is '___'. Can everyone say that with me? Excellent! Now, let's look at this picture/object. What do you see? That's right; it is '___'. This picture/object helps us understand what '___' means.

Teacher: Now, let's try something fun. I will say the new word and want you to repeat it after me. It's a game we call 'my turn', 'your turn'. Ready? '___'.

[Children repeat the word.]

Teacher: Great job! Now, let's clap the syllables of our new word '___'.

[Teacher models first, clapping the word with the corresponding amount of syllables, then the children copy. Next, the children and teacher clap the word's syllables together.]

Teacher: Well done! Now, let's think about what these words remind us of.

[Teacher links the word to a child's prior experiences.]

Teacher: Fantastic! Connecting our new words to our own experiences, we can understand and remember them better. Remember, all the adults in our school will use these words and their meanings so that you will hear them a lot. It will help us remember them.

[Teacher repeats the process with the second new word.]

[Teacher concludes the Unveil stage by summarising the new words and their meanings.]

Teacher: So, our new words today are '____' and '____.'

KEY TAKEAWAYS

- The Unveil stage of the GUIDE model emphasises introducing new words to students, focusing on providing context and making connections to existing knowledge.
- Creating a multisensory learning experience is critical during this stage. Using visuals, real-life objects, actions and tastes can help students make meaningful connections and associations with new vocabulary. It is crucial to engage other senses when a word cannot be easily represented pictorially.
- Consistent use of new vocabulary in different contexts and across all practitioners helps solidify understanding and recall.
- Tying new vocabulary to students' experiences can enhance their comprehension and recall. It can help students form meaningful associations and provide a practical context that aids in their understanding of the new words.

Pause for Reflection

How can you foster a shared understanding among all practitioners to ensure consistent use of new vocabulary across different contexts? Finally, what opportunities can you identify in your teaching practice to connect new words to your students' prior experiences, making their vocabulary acquisition more meaningful and contextually relevant?

INTERACT

The 'Interact' stage of the GUIDE model is where the magic of vocabulary learning truly comes alive. This stage is about active engagement, practice and reinforcement of the new vocabulary words that have been unveiled. It is where the children begin to use the new words in context, understand their meanings more deeply and start incorporating them into their everyday language.

Oral practice is a crucial component of vocabulary acquisition. It allows children to use the new words in context, which helps solidify their understanding and recall. According to a report by the National Early Literacy Panel (NELP) in the USA, oral language development in the early years is a strong predictor of reading success later in life.

More recent research by Hopman and MacDonald (2018) in Psychological Science supports this, suggesting that production practice involves speaking exercises and immediate feedback, which can enhance students' ability to speak and understand the language. The National Reading Technical Assistance Center (2010) also emphasises the importance of repetition and multiple exposures to vocabulary items in learning. Teachers can help children make this critical connection between spoken and written language by facilitating the oral practice of new vocabulary words.

Sentence frames or starters are incredibly effective in the vocabulary teaching toolkit. They provide a supportive structure that guides children in constructing sentences using new vocabulary words. This scaffolding technique is particularly beneficial for children in the early stages of sentence formation or who may find it challenging to incorporate new words into their spoken language.

Consider the sentence frame 'I feel ____ when ____'. This frame can be used to introduce words that express emotions or feelings. If the new word is 'excited', the sentence could be completed as 'I feel excited when I go to the park'. It helps children associate the new word with a personal experience, making it more meaningful and memorable.

In addition to providing a supportive structure for sentence formation, sentence frames also offer opportunities for differentiation. More complex sentence frames can be introduced for children who are more confident or advanced in their language development. For example, the sentence frame 'Although ____, ____' can introduce contrasting or contrasting words. If the new word is 'fragile', the sentence could be completed as 'Although the vase looks strong, it is very fragile'.

Peer practice is another effective strategy for reinforcing new vocabulary. It allows children to practise using the new words and the teacher to observe and circulate. It provides opportunities for immediate feedback, which is crucial for vocabulary acquisition. When children misuse a new word, immediate feedback can help them correct their errors and learn the correct usage.

It aligns with the findings of a research synthesis on vocabulary instruction, which, although conducted with older students, emphasises the importance of active engagement and immediate feedback in vocabulary learning (National Reading Technical Assistance Center, 2010). Recent research also supports this, showing that students in synchronous learning settings reported more peer-centred activities such as feedback, suggesting the importance of these practices in vocabulary acquisition (Fabriz et al., 2021).

Training pupils in peer practice is a crucial step in ensuring its effectiveness. Children need to understand not only what to do, but also how to do it in a way that is respectful and supportive. It is where the role of the teacher and teaching assistant becomes essential. When initiating peer feedback within your classroom, model with your TA what 'kind and helpful' peer interaction looks like, setting clear expectations for behaviour during peer practice activities.

For instance, before initiating a 'pair and share' activity, the teacher might demonstrate how to give and receive feedback with the teaching assistant. They could model how to listen attentively, respond positively and provide constructive feedback. They might also demonstrate what not to do, such as interrupting, dismissing others' ideas or giving unkind feedback.

The teacher could use phrases like, 'I noticed that you used the word "enormous" correctly in your sentence; well done!' to model positive feedback. It is also essential to discuss with the children what unkind feedback might look like and why it is not helpful.

By setting these expectations and modelling respectful, supportive peer interaction, teachers can create a positive learning environment where children feel safe to take risks, make mistakes and learn from each other. It enhances the effectiveness of peer practice in vocabulary acquisition and develops a classroom culture of mutual respect and collaborative learning.

Games and activities can make vocabulary practice more engaging and fun for children. They can turn a task into a fun and exciting challenge. It can be particularly effective for younger children, who learn best when actively engaged in the learning process. Games and activities can also provide additional opportunities for repetition and reinforcement, vital vocabulary acquisition components.

While the list of games provided below offers a variety of ways to engage children in vocabulary acquisition, it is essential to remember that the suitability of each game can vary depending on the specific context of your class. Factors such as the children's vocabulary knowledge, language development and general classroom dynamics can all influence which games will be most effective. Therefore, it is crucial to consider these factors and adapt the games as necessary to best meet the needs of your pupils.

In Reception, most children are still developing their reading skills and cannot yet read fluently. Using pictures or symbols to represent the words alongside the written text is recommended to support their understanding and engagement in the games.

There are various ways to incorporate images alongside words. In my practice, I used the school resource of widget software to provide recognisable images next to each word. However, other teachers may prefer different methods.

The key is to maintain consistency in the images used for each word. Pupils must always see the same image alongside a particular word rather than seeing multiple different images or symbols to represent the same word. This consistency helps to reinforce the association between the word and its meaning, supporting the children's understanding and recall of the new vocabulary.

Vocabulary Game Ideas

Word Detective In this game, the teacher provides clues about a word and the children must guess what it is. This game encourages children to recall the meanings of words and use their problem-solving skills.

Charades Children take turns acting out a word without speaking, while the rest of the class tries to guess the word. This game helps children associate words with actions and reinforces their understanding of the words.

Word Bingo Create bingo cards with vocabulary words. The teacher calls out definitions and the children must match them to the words on their cards. This game helps children recall the meanings of words in a fun and competitive setting.

Pictionary Like charades, but the children draw the word rather than acting it out. This game helps children associate words with images, reinforcing their understanding and recall.

Storytelling Circle Each child adds a sentence to a story using a new vocabulary word. This game encourages children to use new words in context and fosters creativity.

Word Wall Ball Toss a ball around the circle. When a child catches the ball, they have to say a word from the word wall and what it means. This game encourages active recall of vocabulary in a fun, physical way.

Choose the Right One Present the children with different objects or pictures. Say a vocabulary word and the children must choose which object or picture represents that word. Ask the children to explain why they chose that particular object or picture to deepen their understanding. This game tests their vocabulary recall and encourages them to articulate their understanding of the words.

Mystery Bag This game adds an element of suspense and excitement to vocabulary practice. Place an object that represents a vocabulary word in a bag. Give the children clues about the word; they must guess what is in the bag. This game encourages children to think critically about vocabulary words and their meanings, and the mystery element makes the learning process more engaging.

Word Thoughts This game encourages children to make connections between vocabulary words and their experiences or knowledge. Start by giving an example that uses a vocabulary word, such as 'The leaves are "crunchy".' Then ask the children, 'Can you think of something else that's crunchy?' This game helps children understand that vocabulary words can apply to various things and encourages them to think creatively about using them.

Example Interact Script

Teacher: During this part of the lesson, we will have lots of fun using the new words we just learned and some of the words on our word wall, too! Are you ready?

Teacher: Awesome! You are all vocabulary stars! Now, let's use one of our new words in a sentence. 'The ____ is ____.' Partner 1, your turn first. Then, Partner 2 feed back.

[Teacher circulates and listens to peer feedback.]

Teacher: Excellent job. Who would like to share?

[Repeat, swapping partner roles and repeat with the other vocabulary taught.]

Teacher: Fantastic! Now, let's move on to today's game. Today, we are going to play 'Word Detective'. In this game, I will give you clues about a word and you have to guess which of our words is on the word wall. Are you ready? When you think you know the word, raise your hand but do not say it out loud!

[Teacher starts the game by giving clues for the first word. Teacher waits until most of the class have their hands up.]

Teacher: Well done, detectives! 1, 2, 3 – let's say the word all together! '____.' You all did an amazing job using your thinking skills to find out the mystery word. Let's try another word.

[The teacher repeats the process but this time uses one of the new words taught.]

Teacher:	Now, for our final Interact activity, let's pair up and share a story using these new words. You and your partner will take turns adding sentences to the story, trying to use both '____' and '____'. Remember, we want to use kind and helpful words when giving feedback to our partners.
	[Teacher provides a model of how to give feedback with the teaching assistant.]
Teacher:	All right, let's begin our stories!
	[Teacher walks around the room, listening to the stories and providing feedback and encouragement.]
Teacher:	Wow! I have heard some amazing stories filled with our new words and many words on the word wall. Well done!
	[The teacher ends the Interact stage by congratulating the students on their work and reminding them to keep practising the new words.]

KEY TAKEAWAYS

- The Interact stage of the GUIDE model involves active engagement, practice and reinforcement of new vocabulary.
- Oral practice is pivotal in vocabulary acquisition and future reading success.
- Sentence frames or starters are a significant tool in vocabulary teaching, providing a supportive structure for students in sentence construction using new vocabulary words and allowing for differentiation based on students' language development.
- Peer practice is a valuable strategy to reinforce new vocabulary, allowing immediate feedback and correction.
- Engaging students with vocabulary games and activities makes learning more fun and meaningful.
- Consistent use of images alongside words helps reinforce the association between a word and its meaning, aiding students' understanding and recall of new vocabulary.

Pause for Reflection

Consider the diversity of language proficiency levels in your classroom. How might the techniques discussed in the Interact stage of the GUIDE model be adapted to ensure that all students are actively engaged and supported in their vocabulary acquisition journey?

Case Study

Miss J. is teaching her new topic, Seasons, to her Reception class. During her PPA time, she has planned two weeks' worth of vocabulary lessons using vocabulary words related to this theme that will build her pupils' knowledge and understanding of the different seasons based on her class's needs.

Gather

To begin the vocabulary lesson, Miss J. starts with the Gather stage, reviewing some previously learned words through flashcards and a quick game of 'Word Relay'. For 'Word Relay', she divides students into teams and gives each team flashcards that contain previously taught words and the corresponding image or symbol.

Students take turns making sentences with the words before passing along the set. This lively activity helps reinforce their understanding of these weather-related terms.

Unveil

Next, Miss J. moves onto the Unveil stage, introducing two new words using visual aids: 'blustery' and 'harvest'. She holds up a picture card with a symbol that she relates to 'blustery' when saying 'blustery'. For 'harvest', she uses a picture of a farmer collecting crops. The class repeats the new words using the 'My Turn, Your Turn' technique several times. Miss J. also connects the new terms to students' prior knowledge, reminding them of the autumn season they just experienced and the vegetables they tasted at a recent harvest festival.

Interact

Students practise using the new vocabulary during the Interact phase. Miss J. begins with oral sentence practice, providing the frame: 'When it is blustery outside_____.' The children work in pairs, each pair member completing the sentence for each other. As the children say their sentences, Miss J. and her teaching assistant circulate the room.

Next, the class plays a round of 'Pictionary', where students take turns drawing one of the vocabulary words learned so far in the unit and having their peers guess. Finally, they partner up to create short stories using at least one of the new words. Throughout this stage, Miss J. circulates to listen, offer feedback and praise, and prompts students to use the words correctly.

Miss J. feels that the vocabulary lesson went well today. The Gather stage helped prime students' minds for learning by activating prior knowledge. Introducing the two new words with visuals and connections to their experience seemed effective based on students' engagement. During the Interact stage, they enjoyed the practice activities and used the new terms, but a few students still needed prompting and feedback for correct usage. Miss J. notes that she should continue reinforcing the new vocabulary across contexts so they become embedded in her pupils' vocabulary.

SUMMING UP

We have delved deep into the interactive vocabulary acquisition process in Early Years education, emphasising how the GUIDE model seamlessly aligns with this process. We have explored the importance of Gathering words, Unveiling meanings and Interacting with new vocabulary and see the immense impact these stages can have on a child's linguistic growth. As we conclude this chapter, let us take a moment to reflect on the essence of this model – it is an integrated, comprehensive approach that encapsulates the dynamic nature of language learning.

The interactive stage of the GUIDE model is the space where children truly get to engage, practise and reinforce the newly introduced vocabulary. The strategies and activities discussed in this chapter, from oral practice and sentence frames to peer practice and vocabulary games, are all intended to help children understand these words more deeply and start incorporating them into their everyday language. However, it is crucial to remember that the effectiveness of these strategies hinges upon a holistic implementation of the GUIDE model.

Understanding the interdependence of all the stages within the GUIDE model is essential. Each stage flows into the next, creating a continuum of learning that optimally supports vocabulary acquisition. Gathering the words builds the foundation, Unveiling helps children understand the words' meanings, and Interacting allows them to practise and embed these words into their spoken language. The value of each stage is amplified when it is seen as part of this interconnected process rather than an isolated step.

In conclusion, the GUIDE model offers a pathway that bridges the journey from discovering new words to their active usage. Every element of this model contributes to building a robust and engaging vocabulary lesson. The effectiveness of each stage is tied to the others, just as the strength of a chain depends on every link. As teachers, our goal is to guide children along this path, providing support, encouragement and immediate feedback along the way.

Pause for Reflection

Reflecting on your current vocabulary teaching practice, in what ways do you already integrate the stages of the GUIDE model – Gathering, Unveiling and Interacting – into your lessons? How can you further refine these processes to meet the diverse needs of your students better, fostering their engagement and deepening their understanding of new vocabulary?

THE GUIDE FRAMEWORK: HOW DO I PLAN A LESSON?

ACTION PLAN

Table 5.2 An Example Script for the Gather Stage of the GUIDE Model

Action	Currently in Place	Next Steps
Ensure a clear system to track when words were last reviewed, aiding comprehensive vocabulary coverage and the effective use of 'spaced retrieval practice'. Create a word-tracking system – e.g., a spreadsheet or journal – to monitor when words were last reviewed.		
Use flashcards in your teaching sessions, each featuring a vocabulary word on one side and a related image on the other. Make two new flashcards daily, ensuring that you develop a large pool over time. Dedicate 3 minutes daily to creating two new flashcards for the vocabulary session.		
Create a 'Word of the Day Chart' and display it in your classroom so it can be regularly referred to.		
Communicate with other teachers and staff about the new words and their meanings. Ensure the new words and their specific definitions are used consistently across all student interactions. This consistency will help reinforce learning and recall of the new vocabulary.		
Set up peer practice sessions where children can practise using the new words and teachers can observe and give immediate feedback. Before initiating peer practice, demonstrate, along with a teaching assistant, how to give and receive feedback effectively and respectfully. Set clear expectations for behaviour during these activities.		
Regularly assess the effectiveness of the vocabulary teaching strategies and make necessary adjustments to better cater to the needs of your students. Take note of the vocabulary words that children are consistently using correctly and those that they are struggling with. Use this information to guide future lessons and reinforce understanding.		

6
HOW DO I TEACH CONCEPT WORDS?

INTRODUCTION

In this chapter, we dive into the intricate world of conceptual words such as 'above', 'early', 'full' and 'half'. These terms, often overlooked in their simplicity, are, in fact, foundational building blocks that profoundly shape a child's perception and articulation of their environment. Conceptual words, or concept words, are the linguistic threads that weave the fabric of cognitive understanding. They are not merely vocabulary items; they represent significant ideas, relationships and patterns that are essential for interpreting and interacting with the world.

Concept words encapsulate abstract ideas and relational understandings, unlike ordinary words that name objects or actions. For instance, 'above' is not just a direction; it embodies a spatial relationship, helping a child understand positional concepts in relation to their surroundings. Similarly, 'early' is not just a reference to time; it conveys an understanding of sequence and temporal relationships, which is crucial for organising events and experiences in a child's mind.

The Early Years curriculum encompasses a broad spectrum of vital concepts for children's cognitive and linguistic development. These include but are not limited to the following.

Position/location Concepts such as 'under', 'over', 'between' and 'behind' help children understand spatial relationships and are fundamental in developing their sense of space and positioning.

Directional and spatial concepts These include words like 'in', 'out', 'on', 'off', 'up' and 'down', which help children understand and describe the location and movement of objects in space.

Temporal concepts Words such as 'before', 'after', 'during', 'then' and 'later' are essential for understanding time and sequencing events.

Quantitative concepts Terms like 'more', 'less', 'many', 'few', 'all' and 'none' help children understand and describe quantity, an essential skill for mathematical reasoning.

Dimensional concepts Terms such as 'long', 'short', 'wide', 'narrow', 'thick' and 'thin' are important for understanding and describing the dimensions of objects.

Mastering these concepts goes beyond mere vocabulary acquisition; it is about equipping young minds with the tools to navigate, describe and make sense of their experiences. When children grasp the meaning of 'full' and 'half', they are not just learning words, but are developing an understanding of quantity, proportion and comparison. These concepts are pivotal in building reasoning skills and a logical framework for learning, particularly in subjects like mathematics and science.

By integrating these conceptual words into their vocabulary, children begin to see and express the world with greater clarity and precision. This linguistic development is critical as it influences cognitive development, impacting how children think, reason and solve problems. Therefore, our goal in this chapter is not just how to teach these words, but how to unlock their full potential as cognitive and linguistic empowerment tools, laying a robust foundation for all future learning and exploration.

We will continue to use the GUIDE process to teach conceptual words. However, it should be remembered that teaching such words has unique elements due to the nature of the words themselves. We will explore the delicate interplay between introducing and integrating these words into a child's burgeoning lexicon, ensuring that each concept is learned, understood and applied.

Just as we have seen in previous chapters, the success of imparting this crucial aspect of language lies in blending both theory and practice. This chapter aims to equip you with the knowledge and tools to transform abstract concepts into tangible learning experiences, fostering a rich and robust vocabulary foundation for your pupils.

KEY TAKEAWAYS

- Concept words are foundational in shaping a child's understanding and expression of their environment.
- Conceptual words represent deeper ideas, relationships and patterns crucial for interpreting the world. They can encapsulate abstract ideas and relational understandings. These words play a pivotal role in helping children organise events and experiences in their minds.

- The Early Years curriculum includes a wide range of essential concepts such as position/location, directional and spatial, temporal, quantitative and dimensional concepts. Mastering these concepts aids in developing reasoning skills and a logical framework for learning.
- The GUIDE process will be used to teach these concept words, acknowledging their unique nature in a child's expanding lexicon.

> **Pause for Reflection**
>
> As you contemplate the impact of conceptual words on a child's cognitive and linguistic development, reflect on how you currently integrate these vital words into your teaching practice. How do you ensure that these words are not just taught as vocabulary, but as tools for shaping a child's understanding of the world?

GUIDE

We will again use the GUIDE framework introduced in Chapter 5 to support the teaching of concepts. As 'Gather' has been detailed in Chapter 5 and the same principles apply to teaching concept words, please refer to that chapter when planning this element of your lesson. 'Demonstrate' and 'Embed' will be discussed in the next chapters.

UNVEIL

Early Years practitioners are generally in a unique and fortunate position in their approach to teaching. Unlike more rigid educational frameworks, Early Years education thrives on a responsive and adaptive teaching style that is less prescriptive and more attuned to the evolving needs of each child and the class as a whole. This flexibility is advantageous when unveiling new words and concepts to young learners.

In this context, selecting words to introduce to the class can be thoughtfully tailored based on the specific needs and gaps in the children's conceptual understanding. Practitioners have the liberty to observe, assess and determine which concept words will most effectively bridge these gaps and enrich the children's cognitive and linguistic development.

This bespoke approach ensures that the introduction of new vocabulary is not only relevant, but also maximally impactful, catering to the unique learning journey of each child.

One fundamental rule detailed in Chapter 5 remains the same when selecting concept words to unveil – do not cognitively overload children. Introduce two words per lesson. This rule can change slightly, but this should be the general rule of thumb.

Selecting Words to Unveil

As we delve into the process of selecting words to unveil in our teaching, it is essential to remember that the choice of words will largely depend on teacher judgement and pre-assessments of the children's current vocabulary knowledge and understanding. While these decisions are nuanced and tailored to each unique classroom environment, examining examples can help guide and refine your thinking and planning.

The examples provided here serve as a starting point, a springboard for your selection process. They are not intended to be an exhaustive list of either words or concepts, but rather a curated collection to inspire and focus your planning. These words have been carefully chosen based on the levels discussed in Chapter 4, reflecting a progression from fundamental to more complex concepts suitable for Reception-age children.

When selecting words to unveil, always have your cohort's context and current understanding in your mind.

In the process of selecting concept words to unveil in the classroom, Early Years practitioners often face the challenge of balancing individual children's needs with the collective knowledge of the class. While in some instances, it might be feasible to assess each child's concept knowledge in some instances individually, educators typically must rely on their comprehensive understanding of the class to make informed decisions about which words to introduce.

The approach to selecting these concepts can vary, and practitioners may employ different strategies based on the classroom dynamics and curriculum requirements. One effective method is to systematically go through the concepts, pinpointing where there are collective gaps in knowledge. Of course, there may be select children who require some additional support, and this will be explored further in Chapter 9.

Alternatively, selecting concepts that align with the topics or books being explored in class can provide a contextually rich and meaningful learning experience that will deepen the understanding of what is being taught.

When exploring a topic like 'The Seasons', concepts such as 'cold' (winter) and 'warm' (summer) can be introduced.

Table 6.1 A Curated Selection of Concept Words for the Unveil Portion of the GUIDE Model

Concept	Level One	Level Two	Level Three
Comparison	Same Different	Old New Equal	Better Worse Close Far away
Movement	Fast Slow Go Stop	Up Down Quick	Forwards Backwards
Order	First Last	Second Third Next	Middle Before
Quantity	Full Empty None	Lots More Some Less	Half Whole Many Several
Size	Big Small	Long Short Tiny Huge	Enormous Wide Narrow Thick Thin
Superlatives and comparatives			Taller/tallest Shorter/shortest Smaller/smallest Longer/longest
Time	Now	Day Night Before After	Early Late
Weight	Heavy	Light	

For a 'Transportation' topic, concepts such as 'fast' (trains), 'slow' (bicycles), and 'above' (aeroplanes) can be incorporated.

When reading a book like *The Very Hungry Caterpillar* by Eric Carle, concepts such as 'small' (caterpillar) and 'big' (butterfly) can be highlighted. It not only aids in vocabulary development, but also enhances the children's comprehension and enjoyment of the story.

During a topic on 'Space' or when reading the book *How to Catch a Star* by Oliver Jeffers, concepts like 'bright' (stars), 'dark' (space) and round' (planets) can be seamlessly integrated into the learning experience.

By choosing contextual and thematic concepts, practitioners can ensure that introducing new words is educational, engaging and directly relevant to the children's ongoing learning journey. This method enriches the learning experience, making it more immersive and impactful.

KEY TAKEAWAYS

- The process of selecting conceptual words to unveil in teaching relies heavily on the teacher's judgement and pre-assessments of their current vocabulary knowledge.
- When unveiling new words, it is crucial to consider the context of the cohort and their current understanding. Incorporating concepts that align with ongoing topics or books in class provides a contextually rich and meaningful learning experience.
- Selecting concept words involves balancing individual children's needs with the class's collective knowledge. Teachers may employ strategies like identifying collective gaps in knowledge or choosing concepts that complement current classroom themes.

Pause for Reflection

Reflect on the methods you employ to assess your pupils' existing vocabulary knowledge. How does this assessment influence your selection of new concept words? Consider if there are more effective ways to gauge their understanding that could refine your word selection process.

Unveiling the Words

Now you are ready to unveil the words. As with unveiling words from topics and storybooks, remember, the entirety of this process should take around 3–4 minutes. The aim is to keep it short, sweet, impactful and, most importantly, fun. The process will follow the same overall guidelines outlined in Chapter 5, with a few minor changes.

When teaching concept words, it is crucial to incorporate visual aids to enhance understanding and recall. We do this by making effective use of symbols alongside the concept words. Using symbols on flashcards when teaching abstract concepts provides a solid pictorial representation that can bridge the gap between the word and its meaning.

Incorporating symbols alongside words in teaching abstract concepts is a prime example of dual coding. Kirschner and Hendrick delve into the practical applications of dual coding in modern classrooms and emphasise how combining verbal and visual information significantly enhances learning, particularly in the context of complex or abstract concepts (Kirschner and Hendrick, 2020).

When we apply this to teaching concept words, dual coding involves using verbal explanations and visual symbols to represent each word. When a child learns the concept of 'heavy', for instance, they not only hear and repeat the word, but also associate it with a corresponding visual symbol, like an image of a large boulder. This dual engagement – auditory–verbal and visual – creates a more robust cognitive representation of the concept. Kirschner and Hendrick's recent work underscores the effectiveness of this approach, highlighting how dual coding facilitates deeper understanding and aids in long-term retention of information.

For example, when teaching the concept of 'fast', alongside saying and writing the word, presenting a symbol like a running cheetah provides a visual representation of the concept. This dual engagement with the word – visually through the symbol and verbally through its pronunciation and written form – allows children to form a more comprehensive understanding. The visual imagery complements the verbal information, creating two cognitive pathways for the children to recall and understand the concept, which is the essence of dual coding.

Many schools use widget software (especially when supporting SEN), creating custom symbols to represent various concepts. Utilising such technology in teaching concept words is highly advisable, as it offers a visually consistent and engaging way to reinforce learning.

Consistency is vital when selecting or creating widgets or symbols. The chosen symbol for each word should be used uniformly across all teaching materials and across the year group where the word appears. It can include flashcards, story maps, classroom displays and digital resources. Consistency ensures that every time children encounter the symbol, they can instantly connect it with the associated concept word, reinforcing their understanding and memory of the word.

Moreover, integrating these symbols into broader classroom contexts, such as thematic displays or story maps, can significantly enhance the learning environment. It provides children with constant exposure to the words and their meanings, allowing for natural and repeated interactions with the new vocabulary.

Building on the techniques outlined in Chapter 5, the initial introduction of a new concept word should follow a structured and interactive approach. Employing the 'My Turn, Your Turn' method is highly effective in this context. The teacher first articulates the word and then the children repeat it, creating a rhythm that aids memory and pronunciation.

During this process, it is crucial to highlight the corresponding symbol for the word, visually linking it with its symbol. This dual representation reinforces the connection between the verbal and visual elements of the concept word, enhancing understanding and recall.

In addition to verbal and visual cues, incorporating physical gestures or signs will further enrich the learning experience. Many educators are familiar with formal signing systems like Makaton, which can be highly beneficial in this context. If a specific sign is known for a word, incorporating it into the teaching process can provide an additional layer of understanding.

This approach is particularly beneficial for supporting students with Special Educational Needs (SEN) while simultaneously aiding the learning of all students.

For example, when introducing the word 'open', use the Makaton sign alongside the spoken word and its symbol.

However, even in the absence of formal signing knowledge, I have found that simple, intuitive gestures can be equally impactful. Gestures inherently carry meaning and can be easily understood by children. For instance, mimicking the action of running when teaching the word 'fast' can help children associate the movement with the concept.

Modelling Sentences

After introducing the concept word, the next step is to model its use in various contexts. Let us take the word 'up', for example. Doing this involves demonstrating how 'up' can be employed in different sentences and scenarios, thereby showing students the practical applications of the word in real-life situations. For instance, you might say, 'The balloon floated up into the sky', 'Can you reach up and touch the ceiling?', 'The cat climbed up the tree', 'I walked up the stairs.' By using 'up' in diverse contexts, you not only enhance students' understanding of its meaning but also encourage them to incorporate it into their language use.

This modelling stage is crucial in reinforcing the concept and demonstrating its versatility. It provides children with tangible examples of how and when to use 'up', thus embedding the concept into their cognitive framework. For young learners especially, seeing the word used in various sentences and contexts helps solidify their understanding and inspires them to experiment with it in their communication.

Incorporating Wider Strategies

Many other strategies discussed in Chapter 5 are equally effective when teaching concept words. One such strategy is incorporating phonology into the learning process. It can be achieved through the clapping of syllables, a method that not only makes learning fun, but also aids in the phonemic awareness of the children. For example, when introducing a word such as 'under', you can clap out each syllable ('un-der'), helping children to hear and feel the rhythm of the word, which in turn supports their pronunciation and understanding.

Another valuable strategy is connecting new concept words to pupils' prior experiences. When a word can be linked to something that children have already encountered or understand, it becomes more meaningful and accessible. For instance, when teaching 'over', you might refer to a familiar game where they jump over a rope or a puddle. This connection not only aids in comprehension, but also makes the new concept more relatable and memorable.

However, ensuring that these connections are natural and relevant is crucial. Forcing connections where none exist can lead to confusion rather than clarity. When a natural link can be made, it significantly enhances the learning experience. However, if no obvious connection is available, it is better to focus on other methods of teaching the word.

KEY TAKEAWAYS

- Using phonological strategies, such as clapping syllables of concept words (e.g., 'un-der' for 'under'), aids in phonemic awareness.
- Linking new concept words to pupils' prior experiences or familiar contexts (e.g., using the word 'over' in the context of jumping over a rope) supports learning. These connections should be natural and relevant to avoid confusion and enhance comprehension, making the concepts more memorable for the children.
- Use symbols on flashcards for abstract concepts, ensuring consistency across all teaching materials to strengthen the association between the symbol and the word, in line with dual coding principles.
- Combine verbal explanations, visual cues and physical gestures or signs to cater to a diverse range of learners, including those with Special Educational Needs (SEN), facilitating multiple pathways for understanding and memory retention.

> **Pause for Reflection**
>
> How effectively are you integrating visual aids and symbols to enhance understanding and recall? Consider the consistency and relevance of these visual aids in your teaching materials. Additionally, contemplate the role of physical gestures or signs in your teaching. How could incorporating these elements not only enrich the learning experience for all students but particularly support those with SEN?

INTERACT

We will now build upon the 'Interact' stage of the GUIDE model, previously detailed in Chapter 5, to focus specifically on the unveiling and active engagement with concept words. The concept words model is very similar to the original. Again, this is where the vocabulary learning really comes to life. Here is where integral oral development occurs – it is a crucial component. It must be carefully planned, particularly as concept words can represent more abstract ideas than the topic or storybook words discussed earlier.

The approach remains grounded in active engagement and practice when introducing concept words. The techniques from Chapter 5 are still highly relevant and effective. However, the nature of concept words, often more abstract, requires a slightly adjusted approach to ensure comprehension and application.

Oral practice remains a cornerstone of vocabulary acquisition, and with concept words, this involves more than just repetition; it is about encouraging children to use these words in contextually appropriate ways.

As in Chapter 5, sentence frames or starters are particularly effective. For the word 'up', a sentence frame, such as 'I look up to see the ____' or 'I walk up the ___', can be employed. It not only aids in sentence formation, but also helps children associate the word with a relevant action or object.

Peer practice takes on a crucial role in reinforcing concept words. Through activities like 'Pair and Share', children can practise using the new words in sentences, providing and receiving feedback from their peers. Here, as in Chapter 5, the teacher and teaching assistant model respectful and constructive peer interactions, setting a positive tone for these activities.

Using games and interactive activities is particularly effective in teaching concept words. Since these words are abstract, turning their practice into a fun and engaging challenge can significantly enhance understanding and retention.

Refer back to Chapter 5 for more details in all these areas.

Physical activity is vital to the EYFS and should be utilised when teaching vocabulary, particularly concept words. Movement and sensory experiences are powerful tools for teaching concept words, particularly those that are abstract. This approach allows children to connect the concepts to their own experiences, using their bodies and senses to understand the meaning of these words.

An effective way to teach concept words is to engage children in activities where they can physically experience the word. This method is beneficial for words that describe actions or states of being. For example, to teach the concept of 'quiet', you could first ask the children to make a noise by shouting or stomping and then ask them to be completely quiet. This contrast between noise and quietness helps them understand the meaning of 'quiet' through their actions.

Another example could be teaching the concept of 'open'. Ask all the children to close their fists tightly and then open their hands. Discussing the difference between closed fists and open hands in a fun and interactive way helps children grasp the concept of 'open' more concretely.

In addition to movement, sensory experiences can be valuable in teaching concept words. This method uses objects that children can touch, feel or see to understand the concept better. For instance, to teach the concept of 'soft', you could use a feely bag containing objects with different textures. Children can then explore the bag's contents, identifying which objects are 'soft' and which are not.

For spatial concepts like 'above' and 'below', you could use a set of boxes or drawers. Ask the children to identify which box is above or below another, helping them understand these spatial relationships through direct observation and interaction.

These physical and sensory experiences are not just about understanding the words in isolation and relating them to the children's personal experiences. For instance, after the activity with the feely bag, children could be encouraged to talk about other things they know that are 'rough' or 'smooth' from their own experiences, such as a pet's fur or the surface of a playground slide.

By integrating these concepts with personal experiences and sensory activities, children can develop a deeper and more meaningful understanding of the words. This method of teaching not only makes learning more engaging and ensures that the concepts are understood in a way that is relevant and memorable to each child. It is a holistic yet explicit teaching approach that combines physical movement, sensory exploration, personal connection and explicit teaching to make learning concept words a rich and enjoyable experience for young learners.

Concept Stories

Another change in the Interaction section of the model when teaching concept words is adding a short story that should be composed by the teacher. These stories are designed to be simple yet effective tools for introducing and reinforcing the concept words.

The Role of Short Stories in Teaching Concept Words

Diverse examples To enhance understanding, the concept word should be related to a range of objects or situations within the story. For instance, a story about the concept of 'fast' could describe a fast-running child, a fast-moving car and a fast-flying bird. This variety helps children understand the broad applicability of the concept.

Clarity of concept The stories provide clear examples of what the concept word is and, importantly, what it is not. This method helps to delineate the boundaries of the concept.

Repetition in context The stories should be structured to repeat the target concept word multiple times within meaningful contexts. For example, when introducing the concept of 'up', the story might involve a bird flying up and up into the sky or a balloon rising up above the trees. This repetition helps solidify the word's meaning in the children's minds.

Simplicity and focus The stories should avoid incorporating other concept words, where possible, to maintain focus on the target word. Additionally, different grammatical forms of the word should be avoided unless they are the specific focus of the lesson.

Effective Storytelling Techniques

Consistency with visual aids Utilising the symbol or widget associated with the concept word during the storytelling can further support understanding. Ensuring this visual aid is consistently used throughout activities reinforces the connection between the symbol and the word.

Use of gestures When narrating the story, using gestures or signs to represent the concepts can aid in comprehension. For instance, physically moving your hands upwards when discussing 'up' can provide a visual cue to reinforce the word's meaning.

Emphasising key words Important words, especially the concept word and any negatives, should be emphasised in the storytelling. This emphasis helps draw attention to the critical elements of the story.

Case Study: Concept Story for 'Old'

In a cosy corner of the Reception classroom stood an old toy box. It was a wooden box, painted long ago, now with faded colours. The children loved the old toy box.

One day, Mrs L., the Reception teacher, sat with the children and said, 'This toy box is old. It has been here in our class for many, many years.'

After talking about the toy box, Mrs L. took the children on a tour around the school to see more old things. They saw an old clock in the hallway, ticking away the time. 'This clock is old, just like our toy box,' Mrs L. explained. 'It has been at this school for longer than you have been alive.'

Then they visited the school library, where there was an old, comfortable armchair. Its fabric was missing in places, showing how many people had sat there to read. 'This chair is old too,' said Mrs L. 'It has been here for many people to sit and enjoy their books.'

They went outside and saw an old tree. Its bark was rough. 'This tree is very old,' Mrs L. told the children. 'It was here even before our school was built!'

Many of the following concept story techniques were used.

Repetition in context The story repeats the target word 'old' multiple times, each within a meaningful and relatable context. The old toy box, clock, chair and tree are all examples that reinforce the meaning of 'old' through their distinct characteristics, helping the children understand and remember the concept.

Clarity of concept The story focuses solely on the concept of 'old', providing clear examples that help children understand what it means to be old. Each item described in the story has qualities that exemplify age, such as the faded colours of the toy box and the threadbare fabric of the armchair, without contrasting it directly with newer objects, which maintains simplicity and focus.

Diverse examples The story introduces the concept of 'old' through various objects found in familiar settings to the children. This range of examples helps the children see the broad applicability of the concept in different contexts, enhancing their understanding.

Simplicity and focus The narrative maintains a straightforward and focused approach, suitable for Reception-aged children. It avoids introducing other complex concept words that could distract from understanding 'old'.

Contextual relevance The story was told to Mrs L.'s class following a lesson about trees, making the inclusion of the old tree in the story contextually relevant. This strategic placement helps children connect their recent learning and the new concept, enhancing comprehension.

Incorporation of previously learned vocabulary Words like 'cosy' were included in the story. These words had been thoroughly embedded in the children's long-term memory in previous vocabulary sessions. Their inclusion reinforces previously learned vocabulary and shows children how different words can come together in a narrative.

Incorporating Interactive Activities

Following the story, brief interactive activities can be introduced to allow children to experience the concept first-hand. For example, after a story about 'up', an activity could involve children reaching up high or stacking blocks up. These activities provide a tangible experience of the concept, helping to embed understanding more deeply. Alternatively, these types of activities could be woven into the continuous provision for children; this idea will be discussed further in Chapter 8.

By incorporating these custom-made stories and activities into the Interaction stage, the learning experience becomes more engaging and effective in teaching concept words. This approach nurtures a deeper and more intuitive understanding of these essential vocabulary elements.

KEY TAKEAWAYS

- The approach to teaching concept words requires active engagement and practice, similar to the techniques in Chapter 5, but with adjustments for their abstract nature. Effective teaching of concept words involves encouraging children to use these words in contextually relevant ways.
- Engaging games and activities are essential for teaching abstract concept words. Physical activities and sensory experiences are emphasised as powerful tools, especially for words that describe actions or states. Connecting these words with personal experiences ensures that the learning is relevant and memorable for each child.
- Creating simple, engaging stories tailored to introduce and reinforce concept words is an effective strategy. These stories should include diverse examples to illustrate the broad applicability of the concept, such as various instances of the word 'fast' in different contexts.
- Stories should maintain a focus on the target concept word and try to avoid including other complex concept words or different grammatical forms of the word unless they are the specific focus of the lesson to keep the narrative simple and focused.

Pause for Reflection

How can you use storytelling in your classroom to introduce and reinforce new concept words? How can you ensure that your stories are engaging yet simple and focused on the target concept? How might you enhance your storytelling techniques, such as the use of visual aids or gestures, to deepen the children's understanding of these concepts?

Case Study

Mr B., a Reception class teacher, skilfully employs the GUIDE model for teaching conceptual words. His unique approach not only engages children in active learning, but also incorporates ongoing assessment to tailor the vocabulary lessons to their needs.

Mr B. begins his lesson by reviewing previously learnt words, using flashcards that include both the words and their corresponding symbols. During this Gather stage, he keenly observes the children's responses, noting any words that they are not yet secure in. For instance, he identifies that the word 'quick' needs further reinforcement and plans to focus more on this word in tomorrow's session, including additional activities in the continuous provision.

While reviewing, Mr B. pays special attention to the children's interests. Having previously noted a strong fascination with public transport among several children, he chooses to introduce the word 'long' through a story about a 'Long Train'. He uses a picture of a train as a visual aid, along with actions and the symbol the children associate with the concept 'long'. This method not only demonstrates the concept of 'long' effectively, but also taps into the children's interests, making the learning experience more engaging and relatable.

In the Interact stage, Mr B. encourages the children to physically experience the concept of 'long'. He sets up a long piece of ribbon on the floor and has the children walk along it. He also uses sentence frames such as 'The train track is long because …', which the children complete in pairs. This interactive approach helps the children understand and use the word in various contexts.

Mr B. understands the importance of connecting conceptual words to the children's personal experiences. He relates the concept of 'long' to familiar elements in their lives, such as the long slide in the playground or the long corridors in their school. This strategy not only aids in comprehension, but also makes the concept more memorable.

Mr B.'s approach, which, while using explicit teaching, is also holistic and child-centred, combines practical activities, storytelling and keen observation for ongoing assessment. By combining explicit teaching with the children's interests and needs, Mr B. ensures that each concept word is not only learned but understood and applied, fostering deep and meaningful linguistic development in his young learners.

SUMMING UP

Reflecting on our exploration of teaching conceptual words in this chapter, we find that the journey mirrors the integrated nature of the GUIDE model introduced in Chapter 5. This chapter has taken us through a specialised application of the GUIDE framework, specifically tailored for conceptual words in Reception classes. We have detailed how two stages of the model – Unveiling and Interacting – play a crucial role in enhancing a child's understanding and use of these fundamental words.

The essence of this chapter has been the focused application of the GUIDE model to conceptual words, a vital part of a child's linguistic toolkit. These methods underscore the importance of introducing words and embedding them deeply in the children's cognition.

Just as in Chapter 5, understanding the interconnectedness of the GUIDE model's stages has been pivotal in this chapter. Each stage builds upon the previous, creating a cohesive and comprehensive approach to teaching and learning. The 'Unveiling' of words sets the stage for deeper 'Interaction', where children actively engage with and internalise these concepts.

Using symbols is a key part of the strategy. It aids visual learning, reinforces consistency and makes the learning process more interactive and engaging for young learners. The ultimate goal is to create a learning environment where every symbol becomes a familiar and understood representation of a concept word, seamlessly integrated into the children's educational journey.

The stories, activities and classroom discussions have all been designed to form a continuous loop of learning, reinforcing the concepts at every turn.

I hope I have offered a nuanced extension of the GUIDE model, specifically catering to the teaching of conceptual words. The chapter highlights that the strength of teaching lies in the integration of all stages, creating a seamless journey from the introduction of a new word to its active usage and understanding. As educators, our role is to navigate this journey, guiding our young learners with clarity, creativity and care, ensuring that each concept word becomes a familiar and understood part of their growing vocabulary.

Pause for Reflection

How will you ensure that each stage of the GUIDE model, particularly the Unveiling and Interacting stages, builds upon the last, creating a seamless and comprehensive learning experience? Consider the effectiveness of your use of visual aids, such as symbols, in making complex concepts understandable and memorable.

ACTION PLAN

Table 6.2 An Action Plan for Practitioners to Assess their Current Practice and Consider their Next Steps in Order to Successfully Implement the Actions of Chapter 6

Action	Currently in Place	Next Steps
Assess the current concept of vocabulary knowledge and conceptual understanding of your students.		

(Continued)

HOW DO I TEACH CONCEPT WORDS?

Table 6.2 An Action Plan for Practitioners to Assess their Current Practice and Consider their Next Steps in Order to Successfully Implement the Actions of Chapter 6 (*Continued*)

Action	Currently in Place	Next Steps
Use flashcards in your teaching sessions, each featuring a vocabulary word on one side and a related symbol on the other. Make two new flashcards daily, ensuring you develop a large pool over time. Dedicate 3 minutes daily to creating two new flashcards for the vocabulary session.		
Use physical gestures or signs, like Makaton, to represent concepts during teaching. Ensure consistency in physical gestures within all teaching staff.		
Communicate with other teachers and staff about the new concept words and their meanings. Make sure the new words and their specific definitions are used consistently across all interactions with students. This consistency will help reinforce learning and recall of the new vocabulary.		
During planning and delivery, ensure connections are made to new concept words to pupils' prior experiences or familiar contexts to make the concepts more relatable and memorable.		
Pre-write concept stories for concept words being taught, ensuring that each concept word is used at least three times in different contexts. Use clear and simple sentences to maintain focus on the concept words.		
Regularly assess the effectiveness of the concept vocabulary teaching strategies and make necessary adjustments to better cater to the needs of your students. Take note of the vocabulary words that children are consistently using correctly and those that they are struggling with. Use this information to guide future lessons and reinforce understanding.		

7
TALK, TALK, TALK: HOW CAN I MAKE EVERY WORD COUNT?

INTRODUCTION

In Early Years education, particularly in Reception classes, talk's power cannot be overstated. Through my years of teaching in various settings, a consistent observation has been the diverse range of language skills with which children enter Reception. Many arrive with language levels below what might be typically expected for their age due to many reasons explored earlier in this book.

While previous chapters have delved into developing high-quality language through explicit vocabulary teaching, it is equally imperative to recognise the significance of continual, rich language exposure throughout the school day. Here is where the role of all Early Years staff becomes pivotal, as they are instrumental in developing an environment conducive to language acquisition. Educators and support staff contribute significantly to nurturing the children's language skills by consistently engaging in meaningful conversations with children.

This chapter highlights the centrality of words in understanding and conveying meaning. It underscores the critical importance of spoken words in the classroom and the impact of creating scenarios that are rich in vocabulary and guided by knowledgeable adults. These interactions are not just about teaching new words; they're about immersing children in a linguistic environment where they can absorb, process and use language in its most natural form.

We will explore the opportunities within the Reception curriculum to facilitate this constant verbal interaction, closely aligning our discussion with the Communication and Language Early Learning Goals. Our focus will examine how everyday activities and routines can be transformed into potent avenues for language development.

Furthermore, the chapter delves into the final two elements of the GUIDE model – 'Demonstrate' and 'Embed'. We will explore how these stages further enhance vocabulary development using words taught within vocabulary lessons, providing practical strategies for educators to demonstrate language use in context and help children embed new words into their active vocabulary.

THE IMPORTANCE OF ORACY

The current focus on oracy in the UK education system is timely and critical. The Education Endowment Foundation (2021) has underscored the value of oral language interventions, suggesting they can yield up to six months of progress. These interventions encompass a variety of teaching activities, such as reading and discussing books with children and employing structured questioning to enhance comprehension. Crucially, these strategies should be woven into the broader curriculum to be effective.

Incorporating spoken language teaching into the heart of the Early Years curriculum is essential. The Early Years Foundation Stage (EYFS) sets detailed requirements for all children's communication and language development by the end of their Early Years, as discussed in more detail in Chapter 2. These guidelines emphasise the importance of developing strong oracy skills as a foundation for future learning.

The Demonstrate and Embed elements of the GUIDE model are pivotal in reinforcing the Communication and Language Early Learning Goals outlined in the EYFS framework.

Demonstrate: This component of the GUIDE model supports the ELG by providing children with models of good language use. Educators demonstrate the practical use of language through reading and discussing books, which enhances listening comprehension – an integral part of Listening, Attention and Understanding (ELG). Structured questioning techniques help children articulate their thoughts and engage in meaningful conversations, thereby fostering the development of speaking skills, as highlighted in Speaking ELG.

Embed: The Embed element solidifies the demonstrated language skills within the children's repertoire through regular use and practice. Educators ensure that language learning is not an isolated activity but a continuous, integrated process by embedding new vocabulary in various contexts and encouraging children to use these words during class discussions, small group interactions and reflective conversations. This consistent practice leads to the kind of progress suggested by the EEF, as children can make gains in their language development equivalent to up to six months of progress.

The Demonstrate and Embed elements advocate for integrating spoken language teaching into the core of the Early Years curriculum.

Table 7.1 The Communication and Language Early Learning Goals taken from the Early Years Foundation Stage Statutory Framework For Group and School-Based Providers

Communication and Language Early Learning Goals
Listening, Attention and Understanding ELG • Listen attentively and respond to what they hear with relevant questions, comments and actions when being read to and during whole-class discussions and small group interactions. • Make comments about what they have heard and ask questions to clarify their understanding. • Hold conversation when engaged in back-and-forth exchanges with their teacher and peers.
Speaking ELG • Participate in small group, class and one-to-one discussions, offering their own ideas, using recently introduced vocabulary. • Offer explanations for why things might happen, making use of recently introduced vocabulary from stories, non-fiction, rhymes and poems when appropriate. • Express their ideas and feelings about their experiences using full sentences, including use of past, present and future tenses, and making use of conjunctions, with modelling and support from their teacher.

KEY TAKEAWAYS

- Research by the Education Endowment Foundation (2021) highlights the substantial progress achievable through oral language interventions. These interventions can result in up to six months of language development progress.

- The EYFS framework (Department for Education, 2021) mandates comprehensive development in communication and language for children in the Early Years. Incorporating oracy teaching within the heart of the Early Years curriculum is crucial, as it lays a strong foundation for children's future learning and aligns with the detailed requirements set out by the EYFS Framework.

- Embedding Oracy through the GUIDE model: the Demonstrate and Embed stages of the GUIDE model play a critical role in reinforcing the Communication and Language Early Learning Goals of the EYFS.

Pause for Reflection

Reflect on how the EYFS Framework (Department for Education, 2021) principles and the Education Endowment Foundation (2021) findings on oral language interventions influence your approach to teaching oracy in your Reception class. How do you integrate effective language models and structured questioning within your curriculum?

GUIDE MODEL: DEMONSTRATE AND EMBED

Within the GUIDE model, Demonstrate and Embed play a crucial role for children. These stages are vital in solidifying the children's grasp of language and must be considered part of vocabulary teaching.

Table 7.2 The Demonstrate and Embed Sections of the GUIDE Model: A Teaching Framework I have Developed to Explicitly Teach Vocabulary in Reception and Key Stage 1

Demonstrate	Model correct usage and pronunciation of vocabulary words. <ul><li>Highlight new vocabulary words during storytime in classroom conversations and during wider learning.</li><li>Set up a recognition system for pupils who correctly use new words in context.</li><li>Use a word wall or vocabulary chart in the classroom to display new words and their images.</li></ul>
Embed	Incorporate a regular review of vocabulary words into daily routines. <ul><li>Assess pupils' vocabulary retention informally.</li><li>Use songs or rhymes to reinforce both new and previously learned vocabulary words.</li><li>Encourage pupils to 'teach' new words to each other or their families at home, creating a further layer of review and repetition.</li></ul>

DEMONSTRATE

Modelling and Highlighting Taught Vocabulary

Adults in Reception have the unique ability to transform virtually any activity into an opportunity for language development. The approach begins with attentive listening and observant engagement with the children. Providing them with the space to express themselves, following their lead in conversations and responding with thoughtful comments rather than questions creates a nurturing environment for language growth.

Incorporating vocabulary that has been explicitly taught in prior vocabulary sessions into these interactions is a crucial strategy. It doesn't mean just repeating words in isolation; it involves skilfully weaving these words into organic conversations with students. It also involves acknowledging and reinforcing the children's use of these words, a subtle yet powerful way to bolster their language development.

To do this effectively, adults must have a good understanding of the words that have been previously taught. This knowledge allows them to seamlessly integrate these words into relevant discussions, reinforcing children's learning.

Furthermore, this approach requires a collaborative effort from the entire educational team. Each member, from teachers to teaching assistants, needs to be aware of the vocabulary focused on in previous sessions. This collective awareness ensures consistency in the language used across different settings within the school, providing children with multiple exposure points to the new words.

High-quality modelling involves demonstrating new vocabulary in context, showing children how these words fit into everyday language. While requiring dedication and reflection from educators, this practice is invaluable in its impact. It helps children understand the meaning of new words and see how they can use them effectively in their communication.

Incorporating explicitly taught vocabulary into storytime is another fundamental aspect of reinforcing language learning in the Reception class. The deliberate highlighting of these words during storytelling sessions gives children a contextual way to connect with the vocabulary they have learned. Drawing attention to these words during storytime is invaluable, whether the vocabulary is pre-taught for a specific story or spontaneously recognised in a different text.

Doing so allows for a deeper exploration of these words within the narrative context. For instance, if the word 'knobbly' has been taught in a previous vocabulary lesson, when encountering the word in *The Gruffalo*, where this word is used to describe a character, the teacher can choose this moment to pause, highlight and discuss. Here, they encourage children to recall its meaning and how it contributes to the character's description. It not only reinforces their understanding of the word, but also enhances their comprehension of the story.

Moreover, in cases where taught vocabulary appears in different texts, it presents an opportunity to discuss these words and their contextual usage. For example, if a word was taught in a vocabulary lesson for a different text and appears in a new story, the teacher discusses how this word helps to create imagery or set the mood in the story.

Referring back to the case study of Mrs E. from Chapter 4, her teaching of 'knobbly' for *The Gruffalo* becomes an asset during her English teaching. Now that the children clearly understand the word, they can engage in meaningful discussions about the Gruffalo's physical characteristics when they encounter it in the story. The discussion cements their understanding of 'knobbly' and contributes to a fuller comprehension of the story.

The strategic highlighting of taught vocabulary during storytime is an essential technique in language development. It aligns with the principles of effective vocabulary teaching, ensuring that words are not just learned in isolation but are understood and appreciated within rich, meaningful contexts.

Developing this style of interaction is a continuous journey involving practice, observation and adaptation. By consistently striving to enrich children's language experiences through thoughtful, responsive and engaging interactions, educators lay the groundwork for robust language development.

It is crucial to ensure the involvement of all children, including those with English as an additional language (EAL) or those who have delayed language development. To achieve this, educators should foster an inclusive environment that encourages non-verbal participation alongside verbal interactions.

Modelling ways of participating without relying solely on language is vital. This approach includes using gestures, visual aids and other non-verbal communication to convey meaning and encourage involvement. Here, using the same gestures and visuals associated with previously taught words is helpful so that all children in the class can use them to communicate.

Additionally, creating opportunities for and praising verbal contributions, regardless of their level of language proficiency, is essential. This balanced approach ensures that every child, irrespective of their language background or developmental stage, feels valued and can engage meaningfully in the learning process.

SETTING UP A RECOGNITION SYSTEM

Implementing a recognition system for pupils who correctly use new words in context can be a highly effective method for encouraging and celebrating vocabulary acquisition in Early Years settings. However, such systems might not be suitable for all contexts, especially in settings where external reward systems are not part of the teaching philosophy. Where appropriate, though, this approach can significantly boost children's language development and confidence.

Setting up a recognition system can take various forms in settings that allow for external reward systems, depending on what resonates most with the children. For example, it could be as simple as a 'Word Wizard' chart, where children get a star or something similar added to the chart each time they successfully use a new word in context. This visual representation of their achievements can be incredibly motivating for young learners.

It is crucial to ensure that this system is inclusive and acknowledges all efforts, whether a child uses a new word independently or with adult support. The primary goal is to celebrate progress and effort in language acquisition, not just the end result. This approach helps build a positive learning environment where children feel valued and encouraged to experiment with language.

However, the suitability of such a recognition system depends mainly on the individual setting and the cohort of children. As an educator, understanding the dynamics and needs of your class is crucial in determining whether this approach will be effective. Some classes thrive with a visual reward system, while others benefit more from verbal praise or other forms of recognition.

USING WORD WALLS AND VOCABULARY CHARTS

Implementing a word wall or vocabulary chart in the classroom is a visually engaging and effective strategy to enhance the language culture of the classroom. This approach celebrates the acquisition of new language and serves as a constant learning tool for the children.

A word wall or vocabulary chart is a living display of the children's growing vocabulary. Each new word, accompanied by its image or symbol, becomes a part of this display. This visual representation of words and their meanings helps reinforce learning and makes vocabulary acquisition a visible and shared part of the classroom experience. Where appropriate, including phonetic markers such as dots and dashes can be beneficial, especially for words whose phonemes have been introduced in phonics lessons. However, educators should remember that some words may contain graphemes that are yet to be covered in phonics instruction.

While younger children may not yet have the skills to read all the vocabulary independently, the presence of these words in their learning environment is still highly beneficial. The word wall contributes to the classroom's overall reading and writing culture, setting a foundation for literacy development.

Moreover, the word wall or vocabulary chart is a constant reference point. It allows children to see and interact with new words daily, reinforcing their learning and encouraging them to use them in their speech and writing. The visual cues, in the form of symbols or pictures, act as memory aids, supporting the children in recalling and using the words they have learned; this aligns with research showing that visual aids like symbols or pictures enhance word retention by providing a visual cue that triggers memory recall (Pearson and Wilbiks, 2021).

Case Study

Ms P. has been a Reception class teacher for three years and effectively implements the GUIDE model techniques to support her class's vocabulary acquisition.

When using the Demonstrate section of the model, she makes sure that she uses as many techniques as possible to enrich the vocabulary in the classroom.

Ms P. ensures that she always integrates previously taught vocabulary into her daily interactions with students, skilfully weaving words into conversations. All team members in the phase are aware of the vocabulary focus, promoting a consistent language environment in the classroom.

In the small world area, Ms P. observes a child playing with figures representing a dad and a baby. She seizes the opportunity to use 'tiny', a recently taught concept word, by commenting, 'The baby is tiny compared to the dad.' When the child agrees, a discussion leads the child to announce they will find a 'tiny cat' to be friends with the 'tiny baby'. This interaction exemplifies how Ms P. integrates taught vocabulary into everyday classroom scenarios.

Recognising the power of modelling, Ms P. demonstrates using new vocabulary in various contexts. During storytime, Ms P. reads *Where the Wild Things Are*, focusing on the word 'mischief'. She revisits this word, taught in a previous session while reading about Max making mischief. The children then talk about times they have made mischief. This moment enriches the children's understanding of the word in the story's context.

Ms P.'s Word Wizard chart is a vibrant display in the classroom, acknowledging children's successful use of new words. She makes the chart as inclusive as possible, rewarding independent and supported vocabulary use. One instance involves a child, with the support of a teaching assistant, using the word 'stir' in a sentence. The girl has been making cakes and verbally describes what she has done. She cannot remember the word 'stir' but used the correct action. The class TA notices this and models the sentence 'I stir the cake mixture', which the child repeats. This effort is celebrated with a star on the Word Wizard chart, visibly rewarding the child's attempt and reinforcing the learning.

Ms P. diligently incorporates the word wall into her daily teaching routine. Each time she teaches a new word during her vocabulary lessons, she immediately adds it to the word wall and its corresponding image or symbol. This practice ensures that the new vocabulary is visually reinforced immediately. The word wall in her classroom is dynamic; she updates it half-termly to align with the current book or topic being covered. However, Ms P. maintains a dedicated section for older words, which she refreshes weekly. This strategy ensures that previously taught words remain in focus and are not forgotten, helping children revisit and reinforce their growing vocabulary regularly.

Through these examples, Ms P. demonstrates the practical application of strategies for vocabulary development, emphasising the importance of adult interaction, context-rich storytelling, and positive reinforcement in language acquisition for young learners.

KEY TAKEAWAYS

- Educators in Reception have a crucial role in using daily interactions as opportunities for language development, skilfully incorporating previously taught vocabulary into conversations and acknowledging children's use of these words. This approach enhances language growth by providing models of good language use and reinforcing learning.
- It is essential to involve all children, including those with EAL or delayed language development, in vocabulary learning. Educators should use gestures, visual aids and praise for verbal contributions, creating an inclusive environment that encourages participation from every child.

- Implementing a recognition system, like a Word Wizard chart, can motivate children to use new words in context. However, the effectiveness of this approach depends on the classroom's dynamics and the teaching philosophy, and it should emphasise celebrating progress and effort in language acquisition.
- Using word walls or vocabulary charts in the classroom serves as a continuous learning tool, reinforcing new vocabulary. This visual representation supports children's recall and use of new words, contributing to a rich language culture in the classroom and aligning with research on the benefits of visual aids in enhancing word retention.

Pause for Reflection

What are your strategies for modelling and reinforcing newly taught vocabulary in your Reception class? How do you ensure that your interactions with children effectively incorporate and celebrate their use of new words?

EMBED

Incorporating Language into Daily Routines

Incorporating regular reviews of vocabulary words into daily routines is a principal strategy in the 'Embed' stage of the GUIDE model. This approach involves weaving previously taught words into various parts of the school day to reinforce learning and encourage usage.

For example, when discussing the day's schedule, a teacher might say, 'We are going to have a "huge" surprise during Assembly', using 'huge' as a callback to a previously taught word. This method reiterates language and inspires children to use rich vocabulary in their daily interactions. It's about creating a language-rich environment where the repetition of these words becomes a natural part of classroom discourse, solidifying children's understanding and encouraging them to use the vocabulary they have learned actively.

Reinforcing children's use of exciting or previously taught words is an effective strategy in the Embed stage. When a child independently uses a vocabulary word, educators should repeat the word and expand on it, acknowledging and praising the child's use of language. For instance, if a child exclaims 'The leaves are rustling!', the adult might respond, 'Yes, they rustle gently in the wind.' This practice not only reiterates the word for the benefit of all the children, but also demonstrates its usage in context, serving as a natural and affirmative way to reinforce and celebrate the child's growing vocabulary.

Informally Assessing Vocabulary Retention

Observing pupils in the Early Years is fundamental to an educator's role – essentially, the bread and butter of our practice. This ongoing observation is particularly advantageous when it comes to informally assessing pupil vocabulary retention. In my teaching context, I employ several strategies:

Conversational observation During casual conversations, I listen for the use of newly taught vocabulary. It might be during a class discussion or even in casual chatter during playtime. Noting which words are used and how they are applied provides insights into each child's comprehension and retention.

Storytime interaction I encourage children to describe scenes or characters using newly learned words during story sessions. I assess their understanding based on how accurately and confidently they use these words in context.

Playtime language use Playtime offers a natural setting for children to use language freely. I observe how they incorporate new vocabulary in their play, whether role-playing, building or engaging in creative activities.

Group activities monitoring Group tasks, such as collaborative projects or group discussions, are fertile grounds for assessing vocabulary usage. Here, I focus on how children communicate together, especially noting if they use newly introduced words and how effectively they are integrated into their conversation.

Using Songs and Nursery Rhymes

Incorporating songs and rhymes into the Early Years curriculum is a highly effective way to reinforce new and previously learned vocabulary words. The approach is not just a teaching strategy; it is deeply rooted in how children naturally acquire and process language. The research of Di Liberto et al. (2020) underscores the significance of rhythmic speech and melody in aiding language development from infancy. Their findings reveal that infants respond positively to nursery rhymes as early as four months, demonstrating children's natural affinity towards rhythmic and melodic speech patterns.

Nursery rhymes and songs engage a fundamental neural mechanism essential for language learning. It aligns with the standard practice of using songs and rhymes in Early Years to teach vocabulary. These songs' rhythmic and repetitive nature makes them ideal vocabulary acquisition and retention tools.

Furthermore, Di Liberto et al. (2023) suggest that activities such as clapping rhythms, singing nursery rhymes and playing rhythm-based games can significantly enhance speech processing. These activities align brain waves with sound waves for better comprehension and provide a fun and engaging way for children to learn new words.

Creating simple songs to the tune of popular nursery rhymes is an effective method for embedding vocabulary in the minds of young learners. By setting new lyrics, particularly those involving taught vocabulary, to familiar melodies, children can more easily remember and internalise these words. When doing this, use the previously taught actions alongside the taught vocabulary.

Here are some examples. Please note that these are examples only. All Early Years settings are unique, and what may be appropriate for some settings may not be for others. When teaching and performing the songs, remember when using vocabulary to ensure that the corresponding actions are used.

Example: Positional Language Song

(Sung to the tune of 'Twinkle Twinkle Little Star'.)

Up **above** and down **below**,

Here we go, to and fro.

Over, under, near and **far**.

Here we jump; there's where you are!

In, out, through and **around**,

Positional words we have found.

Example: Food Description Song

(Sung to the tune of 'The Wheels on the Bus'.)

The apples in the bowl go '**crunch, crunch, crunch**', '**crunch, crunch, crunch**', '**crunch, crunch, crunch**'.

The apples in the bowl go '**crunch, crunch, crunch**' all through the day.

The soup in the pot goes '**bubble, bubble, bubble**', '**bubble, bubble, bubble**', '**bubble, bubble, bubble**'.

The soup in the pot goes '**bubble, bubble, bubble**' all through the day.

The cheese on the board goes '**slice, slice, slice**', '**slice, slice, slice**', '**slice, slice, slice**'.

The cheese on the board goes '**slice, slice, slice**', all through the day.

> ### Example: Vocabulary clapping song
>
> *(Sung to the tune of 'If You're Happy and You Know It'.)*
>
> If you know the word '[word]', clap its beats. *[Clap syllables of the word.]*
>
> If you know the word '[word]', clap its beats. *[Clap syllables of the word.]*
>
> If you really want to show it, if you're smart and you know it, if you know the word '[word]', clap its beats. *[Clap syllables of the word.]*.
>
> For example, with the word 'delicious':
>
> If you know the word '**delicious**', clap its beats.
>
> *[Clap syllables: de-li-cious.]*
>
> If you know the word '**delicious**', clap its beats.
>
> *[Clap syllables: de-li-cious.]*
>
> If you really want to show it,
>
> If you're smart and you can grow it,
>
> If you know the word '**delicious**', clap its beats.
>
> *[Clap syllables: de-li-cious.]*

FAMILIES AND PEOPLE AT HOME

It's important to acknowledge that the interaction that children have with their families from an early age lays a crucial foundation for vocabulary learning, as discussed in Chapter 1. Before children even start in an Early Years setting, families play a significant role in their language development. As educators, it's our responsibility to view families as essential partners in the learning process, integral to the support of word learning.

While encouraging pupils to teach new words to their families is beneficial for vocabulary learning, we recognise that this isn't always feasible. Various factors, often beyond the control of parents or carers, can limit this kind of interaction. These factors might include language barriers, time constraints, work responsibilities, caring for others within the family or a lack of confidence in effectively supporting their child's learning.

While it's true that the more families are involved, the better, it's also important to recognise that participation can vary. Every exposure a child has to a new word is a learning opportunity, and by working together with families, we can increase these opportunities. Even simple interactions and word games at home can make a significant difference.

To facilitate this, educators can provide guidance and resources to parents and carers, helping them more effectively to support their child's language development. By fostering this collaborative approach, we can create a more comprehensive and supportive learning environment for our students.

Families with English as an Additional Language (EAL) often face unique challenges in supporting their children's vocabulary development in an English-speaking educational setting. It is crucial to recognise that a strong foundation in their home language can significantly enhance the learning of English. Therefore, promoting the home language within the family is essential.

Encouraging families to engage in language games and activities in their home language can support children to develop a robust vocabulary in both their native and school languages. This bilingual approach helps strengthen cognitive and linguistic skills, providing a solid foundation for language acquisition. Engaging in vocabulary games, storytelling and conversations in their home language reinforces language skills and fosters a sense of cultural identity and belonging. It is beneficial for children to see their home language valued and utilised as a learning tool, boosting their confidence and motivation to learn both languages.

Building Relationships

Holding regular workshops with parents is a critical component in the overall strategy for enhancing vocabulary learning in Early Years education. In my experience, establishing genuine, trust-based relationships is the foundation for successful engagement with parents. Vocabulary workshops provide an excellent opportunity for educators to connect with parents, explain classroom strategies and guide them on how they can extend this learning at home.

These workshops are much more than informational sessions; they are relationship-building events. Educators foster a sense of collaboration and partnership by inviting parents into the educational process, explaining the methods and rationale behind vocabulary teaching, and demonstrating how this can be supported at home. Such an approach helps parents feel valued and included in their child's educational journey, which is vital for developing strong school–home relationships.

Furthermore, vocabulary workshops provide a platform for two-way communication. Parents can share insights about their child's interests, experiences and challenges, which can be invaluable for teachers in tailoring their approach to each child's needs. Additionally, these workshops can be tailored to address the specific needs of families, such as providing bilingual resources or strategies for parents who speak English as an additional language.

As the child progresses through school, the relationships forged through these early interactions can strengthen, leading to a more cohesive and supportive learning environment. Regular workshops help build a community where educators and parents work together, ensuring the child's language development is supported consistently at school and at home.

Top Tips for Parents

Understand the power of words:

- Explain why words are important for your child's school success.
- Discuss how knowing more words helps reading, writing and understanding subjects like maths and science.

Create a learning partnership with the school:

- Engage with the vocabulary your child learns at school. Use these words at home to reinforce learning.
- Stay in touch with teachers to understand what vocabulary your child is currently learning.
- Help your child understand these words by naturally using them in sentences at home. It's more beneficial to model their usage rather than directly asking your child to define them.

Make learning fun:

- Play simple word games during daily routines. It could be a word-matching game during dinner or a word-guessing game while driving.
- Encourage your child to create fun stories or drawings using new words.

Focus on conversational vocabulary:

- Incorporate new words into everyday conversations. If your child is learning the word 'enormous', you might talk about an 'enormous lorry' you see while out.
- Encourage your child to use new words in their speech.

Use encouragement, not quizzing:

- When your child uses a new word, praise them.
- Avoid putting your child on the spot with direct questions about word meanings.

Incorporate daily word practice:

- Place words your child is learning in visible places around the house, such as on the fridge or a bulletin board.
- Use spare time for quick and casual word games.

Celebrate their home language (for bilingual families):

- If your family speaks another language at home, encourage your child to learn and use words in both languages.
- Play language games or tell stories in your home language.

Encourage sharing vocabulary:

- Motivate your child to share new words they've learned with other family members, enhancing their understanding and confidence in using these words.

KEY TAKEAWAYS

- Regularly incorporating taught vocabulary into daily routines is crucial for reinforcing language learning.
- Acknowledging and expanding upon children's use of new words enhances their language skills. Informal assessments through conversational observations, storytime interactions and monitoring language use during play and group activities provide insights into children's vocabulary retention and comprehension.
- Incorporating songs and nursery rhymes in teaching aids language development. These activities' rhythmic and repetitive nature makes them effective tools for vocabulary acquisition and retention.
- Building partnerships with families, especially through workshops and shared activities, is critical to extending vocabulary learning beyond the classroom. It includes encouraging language games at home, sharing vocabulary learning strategies and recognising the importance of bilingualism for families with English as an Additional Language (EAL).

Pause for Reflection

What is your approach to involving families in your pupils' vocabulary development? How do you communicate the importance of vocabulary learning to families, and what strategies do you provide to support them in reinforcing this learning at home?

SUMMING UP

The importance of creating a classroom culture where talk is not only encouraged but celebrated cannot be overstated. Through this culture, children find their voice, develop their ideas and build the confidence to express themselves.

Demonstrating language in context breathes life into new vocabulary, making it relevant and tangible for young learners. The Embed stage ensures that these words are revisited and utilised, cementing them in children's growing lexicons. This chapter has explored the many ways that teachers can nurture a language-rich environment, from structured activities to spontaneous conversations that reinforce taught vocabulary, all contributing to a culture of communication.

Ultimately, nurturing a culture of talk empowers children to become confident communicators. In a world where communication is a key to success, these early experiences with language and interaction are invaluable. As educators, our role is to nurture this culture, guiding children through their formative years with the power of language.

Pause for Reflection

Think about how you, as an educator, contribute to nurturing confident communicators in your classroom and what steps you could take to enhance this culture of communication further.

ACTION PLAN

Table 7.3 An Example of a Positional Language Song Sung to the Tune of 'Twinkle Twinkle Little Star'

Action	Currently in Place	Next Steps
Organise professional development sessions focused on effective communication strategies with young children. Include practical exercises and role-playing to enhance staff's conversational skills.		
Train staff to follow the child's lead in conversations, using their interests as a springboard for introducing and practising new words.		
Emphasise the importance of listening to children and building on their contributions to foster natural language development.		

(Continued)

Table 7.3 An Example of a Positional Language Song Sung to the Tune of 'Twinkle Twinkle Little Star' (*Continued*)

Action	Currently in Place	Next Steps
Develop and distribute cribsheets with example dialogues and questions that incorporate new vocabulary.		
These cribsheets can guide staff on introducing words in various contexts and maintaining engaging conversations.		
Integrate new vocabulary into routine classroom activities such as morning circles, snack times and transitions. Encourage staff to use the words naturally during these times, helping children to understand and use them in context.		
Communicate with parents about the focus vocabulary, offering suggestions on how to use these words at home.		
Provide simple guides or newsletters with conversation starters and activity ideas for families.		
Organise workshops for parents and carers focused on vocabulary development and effective communication strategies.		
Include interactive sessions where parents and carers can practise conversation techniques and learn to integrate new vocabulary into daily interactions with their children. Offer these workshops at varying times to accommodate different schedules, ensuring that all parents and carers have the opportunity to attend.		

8

HOW DO I MAKE PLAY PURPOSEFUL?

Through the joyful art of play, profound learning can unfold which, when practitioners cultivate through enabling environments, children can explore, discover and articulate the world around them on their terms. Play is the language of childhood. In these moments of unbridled creativity, children use the vocabulary they have been taught and give it new meaning, shaping their understanding of the world and their place within it.

This chapter will delve into the symbiotic relationship between explicit vocabulary instruction and play-based learning in the Reception year. Here, we will explore the intricate ways in which vocabulary teaching enriches the play environment facilitated by educators and the resources available to children. I will illustrate how intentional vocabulary development can significantly enhance children's independent play, deepening the engagement and interaction with the educational materials provided.

Contrary to what some may believe, play is not a break from learning; it is a complex, multifaceted tool that promotes cognitive, social and linguistic development. Play, when facilitated well, can be part of the learning itself. Through play, children experiment with new words in context, applying their expanding lexicon in a manner that is both meaningful and self-directed. This chapter will present strategies for educators to integrate vocabulary teaching into play.

Moreover, I will provide practical examples demonstrating how a rich vocabulary can transform play into a more immersive and educational experience, equipping educators with the knowledge to create a learning environment where play and language support each other, fostering an atmosphere where children can thrive in communication and creativity.

THE IMPORTANCE OF PLAY

Play, as a fundamental teaching practice, supports the entire spectrum of young children's growth, from social interactions to complex cognitive processes. It is particularly true when play is not simply an ancillary activity but an integral part of a rich curriculum, as suggested by Zosh et al. (2018). Playful learning pedagogies, which align with the characteristics of effective learning (Department for Education, 2021), have been shown to increase learning outcomes significantly (Zosh et al., 2018).

Guided play in particular, where the teacher incorporates learning goals into play activities, has been demonstrated to be highly effective. Research indicates that children learn more vocabulary and develop better spatial skills during guided play compared to free play (Fisher et al., 2013; Toub et al., 2018). This method respects the child's agency while ensuring that learning is intentional and directed towards clear educational outcomes (Toub et al., 2018).

As I mentioned in Chapter 2, I often envision my role as an educator as providing a guiding hand on a child's educational journey. While it is essential to encourage independent exploration and discovery, there is also a significant place for structured guidance. Striking the right balance between these approaches is critical.

It is true that there are valid concerns about overly imposing adult objectives on a child's natural learning process. However, with a thoughtful approach that respects and aligns with a child's developmental stage and needs, guided instruction within play can be a powerful tool. By adopting a child-centric approach, we can foster not only a deeper understanding of concepts, but also ignite a child's innate curiosity and bolster their self-assurance in their learning abilities.

COMBINING EXPLICIT TEACHING AND PLAY-BASED LEARNING

As highlighted in Chapter 2, these developmental areas are rightfully emphasised in Early Years education. It is crucial to recognise the importance of the Prime Areas of Development within the EYFS framework, which includes Communication and Language, Physical Development, and Personal, Social and Emotional Development (Department for Education, 2021).

However, my perspective diverges somewhat in terms of the methodologies employed to achieve these developmental milestones. While play-based learning is undoubtedly valuable, I believe that it should not be the sole approach, particularly for certain children.

Play-based learning may not sufficiently address the needs of all children, especially those from less privileged backgrounds. It is important to acknowledge that not every child entering an Early Years setting comes from an environment that has fostered their development adequately. For many, the lack of enriching experiences, limited space or less engagement at home can lead to developmental gaps.

These disparities mean that explicit teaching and direct instruction are essential for some children to ensure that their development aligns with EYFS standards. To assume that all children can equally benefit from play-based learning overlooks the varied circumstances of each child.

Children deprived of certain experiences might not effectively navigate and learn from their environment or develop crucial language and social skills without additional structured learning; this is especially true of children with a vocabulary deficit, as discussed in Chapter 1.

Recognising this diversity in backgrounds and needs is vital to providing an inclusive and effective Early Years educational experience. We have seen how effective this approach is in the explicit teaching of phonics. The New South Wales Government emphasises explicit teaching as one of the key quality practices for effective learning environments (New South Wales Department of Education, 2023)

We must be aware of the reality: some children start their Reception year at a disadvantage relative to their peers. To address this disparity, I advocate for a balanced approach that combines explicit teaching with play-based activities to address this disparity. This strategy ensures that foundational knowledge areas are adequately covered for all children, reducing the reliance on chance for their educational development.

This perspective does not imply that explicit teaching should overshadow the importance of play in the Early Years. Instead, it emphasises that both explicit teaching and play-based learning are equally vital components of the Reception classroom. Each approach plays a unique and complementary role in a child's development and together, they form a holistic educational experience that caters to the diverse needs of young learners. Therefore, it is crucial to integrate both methods, ensuring a balanced and enriching environment for children at this critical stage of their education.

Environments that supplement and enhance explicit daily vocabulary lessons are pivotal in making language learning more dynamic and engaging for children. Play, in particular, stands out as a powerful means to bring new words to life. From my own experience, when children engage with vocabulary through playful activities, their fascination with language intensifies, significantly accelerating their development as word learners, highlighting again the synergistic relationship between play and explicit teaching.

KEY TAKEAWAYS

- Play-based learning, especially guided play, is crucial for children's development.
- Striking a balance between independent exploration and structured guidance is important. A thoughtful approach that respects a child's developmental stage and needs can make guided instruction within play a powerful educational tool, fostering understanding and curiosity.
- Recognising that not all children benefit equally from play-based learning, it is important to incorporate explicit teaching and structured learning to address developmental gaps.

Pause for Reflection

How do you balance play-based learning and explicit teaching in your classroom? How do you ensure that your approach to education caters to the diverse needs of all your students, particularly those who might need more structured learning experiences?

USING PLAY TO REINFORCE TAUGHT VOCABULARY

In a classroom where play reinforces vocabulary, words transcend their abstract nature, becoming tangible tools for exploration and expression. A prime example of this can be seen when integrating play with words from the vocabulary lessons.

For example, the classic Early Years story *The Little Red Hen* offers a perfect opportunity to integrate and utilise words from explicit vocabulary lessons. By setting up specific scenarios within the role play area, children can actively engage with words like 'knead', 'corn', 'cut', 'grind', 'bull' and 'bake', applying them in a context that mirrors both the story and their recent vocabulary learning.

Here, imaginative practitioners can dream up a multitude of themes within the area to provide a hands-on way for children to use the newly learned vocabulary. For instance, part of the role-play area can be dedicated to a bakery where children can 'bake' bread. Here, they would use the word 'knead' as they pretend to prepare dough (Play-Doh could be used), physically mimicking the action to reinforce the word's meaning. Another section could mimic a farm field where 'corn' is grown, allowing children to use the word as they engage in activities such as planting or harvesting.

Thinking back to the previous chapter and the importance of 'talk', it is also an excellent opportunity for adults to engage in both play and reinforcing vocabulary, enhancing the learning experience for children. For example, in the bakery section, educators can actively participate by guiding children through 'baking bread'. They can demonstrate how to 'knead' the dough, using the word in sentences and asking children open-ended questions that encourage them to use the vocabulary independently. This interactive demonstration helps children understand the word's meaning and context through observation and physical participation.

Educators can join the children in planting or harvesting activities in the farm field area, where 'corn' is featured. As they engage with the children, they can use the word 'corn' in various sentences, enhancing the children's understanding of the term. Educators can guide the children in creating small narratives or scenarios around the corn-growing process, making the activity both educational and entertaining.

A mini mill within the play area can be where children 'grind' wheat into flour. By turning cranks and pretending to operate mill machinery, they learn what 'grind' means and how it fits into the process of making bread. The presence of a toy 'bull' in the farm setting can lead to discussions and play scenarios involving farm animals, further enhancing their understanding of different roles within a farm.

Of course, it is important to note that not all these themed areas need to be created simultaneously, nor is it necessary to use every single one. The key takeaway is the multitude of ways taught vocabulary can be utilised to enrich role-play areas.

The examples provided are just a few possibilities among many, illustrating the versatility and adaptability of vocabulary in enhancing children's play experiences. The goal is to showcase the diverse methods that educators can employ to integrate newly learned words into various playful contexts, thereby reinforcing language learning dynamically and playfully.

KEY TAKEAWAYS

- Using play to reinforce taught vocabulary transforms words into tangible tools for children. Guided play supports children to create interactive scenarios where children can apply words in context.
- Setting up thematic areas based on vocabulary taught allows children to engage with new vocabulary in a hands-on manner.
- Educators play a crucial role in enhancing learning by participating in play scenarios. Their involvement includes demonstrating actions, using vocabulary in sentences and asking open-ended questions that encourage children to use the words independently.

Pause for Reflection

Reflect on how you currently integrate taught vocabulary into play-based activities in your classroom. Consider ways you might enhance or adapt your current strategies to further support children's vocabulary development through play. What additional thematic play areas or scenarios could you introduce that would align with recent vocabulary lessons?

Case Study

In Mrs R.'s Reception class, the magic of purposeful play comes to life, blending explicit vocabulary instruction with playful learning experiences. Mrs R., a dedicated educator, has masterfully created an environment where play is not just an activity but a language of learning, beautifully intertwining with the vocabulary lessons.

During their term two topic, 'Space', the children find exploring space becomes an immersive learning adventure. After some vocabulary lessons teaching them keywords relating to the topic that Mrs R. has pre-planned, the children can use them when engaging with the environment.

Mrs R. has transformed a section of the classroom into a miniature spaceship, and the environment allows children to engage with words like 'rocket', 'astronaut' and 'planet'. Mrs R. enhances children's vocabulary acquisition by asking open-ended questions during play. These questions prompt children to use newly learned terms like 'rocket' and 'astronaut' in their speech, encouraging them to think creatively and articulate their ideas.

For example, while a child pretends to be on a rocket, they might say, 'My rocket will fly in orbit around the Earth.' Mrs R. asks, 'How will your rocket move in orbit?' The child responds, 'It will whizz through space.' Mrs R. is pleased as 'whizz' was another of the vocabulary words she has taught.

Integrating play with previously taught vocabulary exemplifies high-quality modelling, encouraging children to use new words contextually and effectively in their communication. Such questions stimulate imaginative responses, embedding vocabulary in meaningful and engaging dialogue.

The space theme is brought to life with the help of Miss Gino, a teaching assistant (TA), who creatively crafts astronaut hats for the children. They use these in the moonlike play area, engaging in a simulated journey to the moon. Miss Gino, guided by the crib-sheets developed by Mrs R. in her weekly planning, facilitates this play effectively. She uses specific space vocabulary, like 'launching' for the rocket's takeoff and 'floating' to describe zero gravity. This targeted approach helps children grasp and use new vocabulary in an engaging, context-rich environment.

In Mrs R.'s Reception class, purposeful play and explicit vocabulary instruction are harmoniously blended. Children apply new vocabulary with Mrs R. and Miss Gino

> facilitating and enhancing learning through open-ended questions and bespoke activities. Their approach, guided by Mrs R.'s carefully crafted cribsheets, effectively embeds vocabulary in a context-rich, imaginative play environment, demonstrating the power that play can have when guided and supported by prior explicit teaching.

ENABLING VOCABULARY-RICH PLAY ENVIRONMENTS

In developing vocabulary-rich play environments, it is essential to recognise that while some children naturally engage in interactive and imaginative play, others may benefit from additional support and structure. One effective strategy is to have a thematic play corner that changes regularly and naturally encourages interaction and language use.

For instance, turning a corner of the classroom into a mini hospital, complete with a reception desk, waiting area and patient beds, can introduce children to a new vocabulary related to health, professions and care. Educators can introduce new words specific to this scenario, such as 'stethoscope', 'appointment' or 'patient', by incorporating new words via quick one-to-one direct teaching framed as a discussion. Here is also where the crib sheets with example dialogues and questions incorporating new vocabulary for support staff, as discussed in Chapter 7, come in handy.

Scripting Play

Play scripts are an excellent resource for language development in the classroom, providing a structured yet flexible framework for imaginative play. These scripts offer simple, guided scenarios that introduce new vocabulary and encourage role-playing and storytelling. Play scripts can be beneficial for support staff in the classroom as they provide a clear structure to engage with children in a meaningful and educational manner.

For instance, a play script centred around a day at the zoo can be an engaging way to introduce children to various new words and concepts. In this scenario, children can take on roles such as zookeepers, tour guides or visitors. The zookeeper might talk about animals' different 'habitats', using the word in context to describe where each animal lives. A child playing the tour guide could use words such as 'species' to explain the types of animals in the zoo and 'conservation' to discuss how the zoo helps protect animals.

Furthermore, play scripts can be adapted to various themes and interests of the children. For example, a script about a space mission could introduce terms such as 'astronaut', 'rocket', 'orbit' and 'galaxy'. Children could role-play a journey to the moon or a space station, using the new vocabulary in context as they navigate their imaginary space adventure.

Play scripts also allow for creativity and improvisation. While the script provides a basic storyline and key vocabulary, children and staff can expand on the narrative, adding their own ideas and words. This flexibility makes play scripts a dynamic tool for language development.

Play scripts are particularly effective in small group settings, which has been evident in my teaching experience. Children are enthusiastic about participating in these scripted plays and often express eagerness and anticipation for the next opportunity. This excitement is a testament to how much they enjoy and value these activities. Through play scripts, children not only get the chance to reinforce and practise new vocabulary, but they also engage in performance, which significantly contributes to developing their oracy skills from a young age.

Performing in a play script allows children to articulate words and phrases in a structured context, enhancing their speech and communication abilities. It is a fun and engaging way for them to practise speaking in front of others, boosting their confidence and linguistic competence. Additionally, these scripts provide an excellent platform for children to express themselves, explore different roles, and collaborate with peers, further fostering their social and emotional growth.

Moreover, play scripts can be a valuable resource for parents as well. Sending these scripts home, along with a brief explanation, encourages family involvement in the child's learning process. The structured nature of these scripts makes it easy for parents to understand and engage with the educational content, further reinforcing the vocabulary and concepts introduced in the classroom.

By using play scripts, educators can support children in developing their vocabulary and social, emotional and cognitive skills.

Case Study: Play Script

In Mr C.'s Reception class, play scripts are a key tool for enhancing language development. For instance, in their 'Gardening' topic, Mr C. created a script called 'The Garden Adventure' to introduce and reinforce new vocabulary.

The children have already had a week's worth of vocabulary sessions and have encountered all the words used in the script. However, Mr C. knows the importance of cognitive load theory and retrieval practice. So, he begins by discussing the script's characters and words with the children, reinforcing their meaning through simple and fun questioning. This preparatory discussion ensures that the children feel at ease with the context of the words they will be using.

During the script's enactment, Mr C. actively guides children through their parts as Gardener, Butterfly, Bee and Flower. He prompts them with open-ended questions like, 'What do you think a flower needs to grow?' This interactive approach makes the learning experience more engaging and effective. He also encourages children to add their ideas to the script, fostering creativity and deeper engagement with the vocabulary.

By using this script, Mr C. helps children practise new words and enhances their storytelling and oracy skills. He makes the script available to parents, extending learning beyond the classroom and involving families in reinforcing the vocabulary at home. This holistic approach demonstrates the power of play scripts in fostering language development in young learners.

Title: The Garden Adventure (based on a gardening topic)

Vocabulary words from current topic:

- bloom
- dig
- shiny
- seed
- soil
- petals
- leaf
- roots
- grow

Vocabulary words from previous topics:

- strong
- tall
- adventure
- new
- beautiful

Characters:

- Gardener
- Butterfly
- Bee
- Flower

Script:

Gardener (holding a watering can): Good morning, beautiful garden! Let's **dig** around the **soil** and help our **seeds** grow.

Butterfly (fluttering around): Hello, Gardener! I see some **shiny** leaves on that plant. They look so healthy!

Bee (buzzing near a flower): I'm here to help the flowers **bloom**. Their **petals** will open up.

Flower (played by a child standing still with arms stretched out like petals): I feel **strong** and **tall** today. Thank you for watering my **roots**, Gardener.

Gardener: Of course! A garden is all about helping things **grow**. Let's see which plants will **bloom** next.

Butterfly: I can't wait to see the **new** flowers. I bet they will be as **shiny** as these leaves.

Gardener: Every day is an adventure here. Let's keep taking care of our garden, watching our seeds turn into **beautiful** plants!

Using Props

Incorporating props like microphones and a DIY television into role-play areas often leads to delightful and unexpected uses by children, demonstrating their creativity and capacity for imaginative play. For instance, I recall a memorable moment when one child took on the role of a YouTube influencer, complete with a make-believe channel dedicated to 'How to Be a Good Teacher'. This inventive idea led to an enthusiastic request to interview the headteacher, an opportunity we eagerly facilitated.

Beyond microphones and television sets, there are numerous other props that can be used to stimulate language development. For example, using toy mobile phones can encourage dialogues and conversations, where children can practise greetings, farewells and simple enquiries, integrating words like 'hello', 'goodbye' and 'how are you?'.

Dress-up costumes hold a special place in the Early Years classroom, serving as a catalyst for imaginative and vocabulary-rich role-playing scenarios. The key to maximising their educational potential lies in aligning these costumes with the vocabulary that children have recently learned. While budget constraints are a valid consideration, creatively crafted DIY costumes made by the Early Years team can be remarkably effective and impactful.

For instance, after vocabulary lessons on animals, creating simple animal head-bands using coloured card, googly eyes and glue can be a delightful way for children to engage with relevant vocabulary.

Costumes need not be elaborate to be effective. A cape made from a piece of old fabric can turn a child into a superhero, where they can use words like 'rescue', 'brave' and 'fly'.

Similarly, a cardboard crown can transform a child into a king or queen, encouraging them to use royal vocabulary such as 'throne' or 'rule'.

They provide an opportunity for staff to engage with children in a playful yet educational manner, guiding their play towards meaningful and language-rich experiences.

A puppet theatre can be another excellent addition, where children can narrate stories or enact scenarios using puppets, thus practising narrative skills and new vocabulary in a storytelling context.

Props like maps and globes can introduce geographical vocabulary and concepts, allowing children to talk about different countries, oceans and landmarks. Similarly, construction sets or building blocks can be used to discuss concepts related to architecture and engineering, using words like 'build', 'balance' and 'design'.

In the example of the child acting as a YouTube influencer and interviewing the headteacher, such role-play not only reinforced vocabulary related to education and teaching, but also provided a platform for practising public speaking and interview skills. This interaction showcases how props can extend beyond mere playthings and become instrumental in developing communication skills, creativity and confidence in using new words.

KEY TAKEAWAYS

- Play scripts offer structured scenarios for imaginative play, helping children practise and understand new vocabulary. These scripts can be tailored to various themes, such as a zoo or a space mission, allowing for creative exploration while learning new words.
- Props like microphones, toy phones, dress-up costumes, puppets and other items enrich the role-playing experience, encouraging imaginative use of vocabulary. Props help create realistic scenarios where children can practise using new words in meaningful contexts.

Pause for Reflection

Consider how play scripts and props could be introduced into your learning environment to stimulate language development further. How can you creatively adapt your existing resources to create more immersive and language-rich play experiences for your children?

SUMMING UP

I hope this chapter underscores the profound impact of play in the Early Years of education, particularly in enriching language development and vocabulary acquisition. There is a deep symbiotic relationship between explicit vocabulary instruction and play-based learning; these elements work harmoniously to develop a rich learning environment.

We have explored how structured play activities, such as role-playing with dress-up costumes or engaging with play scripts, not only encourage the use of new words and enhance social, emotional and cognitive skills. These activities, when integrated with explicit teaching, create a balanced approach, ensuring that all children, regardless of their background, have the opportunity to thrive.

It reiterates the importance of adult involvement in play. Joining in with children's play is crucial, allowing adults to model language use and engage in reciprocal communication. This kind of involvement supports language development and enriches the play experience, making it more meaningful and enjoyable for children.

By thoughtfully designing play environments and incorporating interactive elements, educators can create spaces that naturally promote language development and vocabulary acquisition, catering to the diverse needs of all children in the classroom.

It is clear to me that the intentional combination of play and structured vocabulary lessons is a powerful strategy in early childhood education. It cultivates an atmosphere where children can thrive in both communication and creativity, laying a solid foundation for their future learning journey. So, I hope I have inspired you to embrace the joy and educational value of play, guiding children towards a love for words and a passion for learning that will accompany them throughout their educational journey.

Pause for Reflection

How do your play-based activities complement and reinforce the explicit vocabulary lessons? Are there opportunities to deepen this integration? What are your next steps?

ACTION PLAN

Table 8.1 An Action Plan for Practitioners to Assess their Current Practice and Consider their Next Steps in Order to Successfully Implement the Actions Described in Chapter 8

Action	Currently in Place	Next Steps
Systematically evaluate the classroom and other learning environments to assess how effectively they support vocabulary development.		
When planning vocabulary lessons, concurrently design classroom play areas that will reinforce the new vocabulary. Consider how different areas in the classroom can be themed or equipped to encourage the exploration and application of these words.		
Regularly rotate and update themes (in line with your usual classroom updates) in these areas to reflect the vocabulary being introduced in recent lessons, ensuring that the environment stays dynamic and closely tied to the vocabulary.		
Plan for guided play activities where teachers can focus on vocabulary development.		
Plan for utilising different play scenarios (e.g., role-play, story enactment) to reinforce vocabulary from recent lessons in a tangible context.		
When planning, create simple play scripts that incorporate recently taught vocabulary words.		
Provide guidance for support staff on facilitating role-playing and storytelling sessions using these scripts effectively.		
Share strategies and insights with parents to extend vocabulary learning and play-based activities at home, ensuring a cohesive learning experience.		

9

HOW CAN I EMPOWER EVERY CHILD'S VOCABULARY JOURNEY?

In primary education, particularly the Early Years, it is crucial to recognise and appreciate the diversity in children's learning journeys. We must approach this topic with sensitivity and a deep understanding of individual differences.

This chapter focuses on children who currently require additional support in their vocabulary acquisition, respecting their unique starting points and learning trajectories as outlined in the Early Years Foundation Stage (EYFS) framework (Department for Education, 2021).

Emphasising the importance of an inclusive approach, I will share strategies and practices that address the specific needs of children who require additional support in their vocabulary acquisition. Recognising that every child has unique strengths and areas for growth, the aim is to provide support that empowers children.

We delve deeper into how the direct teaching of vocabulary can significantly contribute to developing oracy skills, especially for children who need additional support. Oracy, the ability to express oneself fluently and confidently in spoken language, is a vital skill that forms the foundation for effective communication and academic success.

By focusing on explicit vocabulary instruction, we provide children with the necessary linguistic tools to articulate their thoughts, engage in classroom discussions and understand the spoken word more effectively.

Based on Rosenshine's Principles of Instruction (Rosenshine, 2012), the chapter will illustrate how structured instructional guidance particularly benefits novice learners in language development. As discussed throughout the book, Rosenshine's principles emphasise the importance of clear, step-by-step teaching, frequent review and immediate feedback – all crucial in helping children build a strong vocabulary foundation. The chapter will explore how these principles can be adapted to specifically target vocabulary, demonstrating that well-structured instruction can lead to significant improvements in language proficiency.

The primary aim of this chapter is to provide educators with insights and tools to effectively support children who need additional help in developing their vocabulary. Through a blend of research-based strategies and practical applications, we will explore how to enhance vocabulary acquisition in a way that respects and nurtures each child's unique learning path in an environment where every child can thrive in their language and communication skills. By doing so, we not only assist them in improving their vocabulary and reading skills, but also contribute to their overall development as confident and capable learners.

LANGUAGE MATTERS

In our discussion of supporting children who require additional support with vocabulary acquisition, it is crucial to address the language used to describe these learners. The terms we choose have significant implications for how children perceive themselves and how others perceive them. While the situation has improved in recent years, a cursory glance at various educational forums and teaching groups on social media platforms, such as Facebook, reveals that labels like 'low' are still used too often. These labels can unintentionally impart negative connotations, potentially impacting a child's self-esteem and eagerness to learn.

These descriptors, even when used casually or with no ill intent, can contribute to a negative mindset for teachers regarding a child's abilities. They can lead to a cycle of lowered expectations and reduced opportunities for growth, both from the child's and the educator's perspective.

This chapter will not refer to the children as 'bottom' or 'low'. The language we use to describe young learners matters profoundly. Terms like 'low', 'lower' or 'lowest' can inadvertently carry negative connotations and contribute to stereotyping and unconscious bias.

We create a more positive and encouraging learning atmosphere by consciously avoiding labels that might limit or define a child's capabilities. I strongly encourage educators across all phases to adopt this mindset, focusing on the strengths and potential of every child. Educators play a vital role in shaping the norms and practices within educational settings, including how we discuss student attainment. By consciously choosing words that reflect the potential and capabilities of all students, teachers set a tone of respect and possibility.

Alongside this, it also changes how children see themselves. Children are very astute in noticing how their teachers perceive them. The language and attitudes we adopt in our educational environments can significantly impact a child's self-esteem and motivation. This shift in language is more than just semantics; it's about creating a culture where every child is seen, valued and understood for their individual abilities and needs.

I advocate using positive and empowering language that acknowledges each child's potential for growth and learning. By shifting our vocabulary, we foster a more inclusive and supportive educational environment and reinforce the idea that every child's learning journey is unique and valuable.

In this book, I am committed to using language that uplifts and encourages, which, in turn, I hope helps you nurture a learning environment where every child is given the respect and opportunity to succeed, irrespective of their current level of proficiency.

KEY TAKEAWAYS

- The language used by educators to describe students, particularly those needing additional support, plays a crucial role in shaping both teacher expectations and student self-perception. Avoiding negative labels like 'low' can prevent a cycle of lowered expectations and enhance students' self-esteem and motivation.
- Adopting a vocabulary emphasising each child's potential and unique learning journey encourages educators to see and treat every child as being capable of growth and learning.

Pause for Reflection

Think about the language you use in your classroom, especially when discussing students who require additional support. How do you describe these learners to colleagues, parents and students themselves?

Children Who Need Additional Support

In any classroom, children benefit from whole-class teaching methods. However, it is equally important to recognise that some students may require additional, more focused help to support their vocabulary development alongside whole-class teaching.

Building Relationships with Parents and Carers

The initial step in providing targeted vocabulary support involves establishing a strong connection with the parents and carers of the children. In the unique context of Reception classes, practitioners often have the advantageous opportunity to meet with parents and carers in their home environments. These one-to-one visits, typically conducted before the school year begins, are invaluable in laying the groundwork for a collaborative relationship.

I strongly advise carrying out these home visits whenever possible. They are instrumental in developing deep and meaningful relationships with the families of the children. Even if your school has an attached nursery where such visits might have already occurred, the transition to a Reception class represents a significant new phase in a child's education. Therefore, these visits remain vital in understanding the child's current needs and setting the stage for their upcoming learning journey.

During these home visits, Reception practitioners gain insights into the child's background, interests and potential challenges they may face. These interactions are not just formalities but integral in understanding the child's linguistic environment and the support they receive at home. Engaging in open and empathetic dialogues with parents and carers allows educators to gather crucial information about the child's language exposure, daily routines and familial interactions, which can significantly influence vocabulary development.

These initial meetings also set the tone for ongoing communication throughout the school year. By establishing a rapport with parents and carers early on, practitioners can develop a sense of trust and partnership. This relationship is essential for creating a supportive network around the child, where information and observations can be shared freely and collaboratively.

The information gleaned from parents and carers can be instrumental in identifying which children may need additional support in vocabulary development. Understanding a child's home language, exposure to books and engagement in conversations at home provides valuable context. It enables practitioners to tailor their support strategies not just to the child's needs in the classroom, but also to complement and extend the language experiences they have at home.

In cases where home visits are not feasible, alternative measures can be taken to ensure that this crucial engagement with parents and carers is not overlooked. If your school has an attached nursery, I suggest arranging meetings with the nursery practitioners. These discussions should aim for a detailed handover, focusing on each child's linguistic development, interests and any specific areas where they may need additional support.

Another valuable alternative is organising one-to-one meetings with parents and carers within the school, akin to a parents' evening. Although you cannot see the child in their home context, it provides a dedicated space for practitioners to learn more about the child. These interactions help gather essential information and signal to the parents and carers that the school is deeply invested in their child's educational progress.

Suggestion Questions/Conversations to Have with Parents

Language exposure at home:

- What languages are spoken at home?
- Can you describe some of the daily conversations your child is exposed to at home?

Interest in books and stories:

- Does your child have a favourite book or story?
- What kind of stories or topics does your child seem most interested in?
- When looking at books, does your child name the pictures? What kinds of things do they typically point out or talk about?
- Can they describe what is happening in the pictures?

Engagement in conversations:

- How does your child communicate their needs or feelings at home?
- How many words does your child typically use in a sentence?

Naming body parts:

- Which body parts can your child identify?

Routine and language use:

- What does a typical day look like for your child and how do they use language throughout the day?
- Are there any specific times or activities when your child is more talkative?
- Does your child talk about their daily activities or experiences?
- What kind of phrases or sentences do they use?

Observations of vocabulary and expression:

- Have you noticed any new words or phrases your child has started using recently?
- How does your child express themselves when excited, upset or curious?

Social interaction and language:

- How does your child interact with other children and adults?
- Can you describe how your child communicates during play with others?
- Does your child use names to identify people they know? Could you give examples of the names they frequently use?
- Are there any familiar adults or children your child refers to by name?

Naming and requesting food items:

- How does your child ask for food or drinks? Do they use specific names for different items?
- Could you share some examples of food-related words your child uses regularly?

Feedback and concerns from parents:

- Do you have any concerns about your child's language development or vocabulary use?
- Is there anything specific you want us to focus on or be aware of in supporting your child's language development?

Assessing the Diverse Language Needs of Children

There may be some children who are verbally expressive at home but hold back at school, perhaps due to a lack of confidence or familiarity with the new environment. These children often possess a rich bank of words but need the right encouragement and support to use them confidently in school.

On the other hand, some children might arrive in the classroom with a limited vocabulary, having been exposed to relatively few words in their early years. This lack of exposure can significantly impact their ability to express themselves and engage with the classroom environment.

Another distinct group within the classroom comprises children for whom English is an additional language. These English language learners might understand the words they hear, but often find it challenging to articulate them. Their needs are unique and require an educator's keen observation and understanding. It is crucial to consider their ability to communicate in English and their proficiency in their home language, as this provides valuable context for their overall language development.

Every school engages in a baseline assessment for children entering Reception, which serves as a crucial tool in understanding each child's starting point in their educational journey. A vital component of this assessment typically includes evaluating vocabulary understanding. This evaluation is not just about measuring the range of words a child knows, but also gauging their comprehension of early developing concepts. By effectively assessing vocabulary understanding, educators gain valuable insights into the language development stage of each child.

It is essential within these baseline assessments to focus on whether children understand fundamental language concepts. These concepts may include basic categorisation (like colours, shapes and sizes), simple verbs (actions they commonly see or do) and everyday nouns (objects and people in their environment).

Identifying gaps in vocabulary understanding through these assessments is critical because it allows for the implementation of early interventions. Targeted support can be put in place promptly. Early intervention is essential in bridging gaps and supporting language development, which is foundational for all other areas of learning.

Assessments are not limited to the start of the Reception year. They can and should be conducted with children who may join the class at various points throughout the year.

Please note, however, that the following guidance outlined in this chapter is designed to enrich children's grasp and utilisation of Level One vocabulary. These foundational elements of language are crucial stepping stones in a child's linguistic development and are pivotal for effective communication and comprehension. The goal of these interventions is to provide children with a robust vocabulary foundation, empowering them with the words and language structures necessary to express themselves and understand the world around them. While these strategies can support vocabulary acquisition, they do not substitute specialised advice and support.

In cases where educators observe significant concerns about a child's speech, language or overall communication development, it is crucial to seek guidance from specialised professionals. Collaborating with the school's Special Educational Needs Coordinator (SENCO) can provide valuable insights into the child's specific needs.

KEY TAKEAWAYS

- Establishing a strong connection with parents and carers is crucial in providing targeted vocabulary support. Home visits by Reception practitioners offer invaluable insights into the child's background and linguistic environment, laying the foundation for a collaborative relationship that extends throughout the school year.
- Regular communication with parents and carers before their child starts in Reception, whether through home visits, nursery practitioner handovers or one-to-one meetings

at school, is essential. Involving parents through targeted questions and dialogues enriches the understanding of the child's language use and development.

- Conducting thorough baseline assessments helps identify each child's language abilities and needs. Early interventions based on these assessments can significantly aid in language development, particularly for foundational vocabulary.

- If serious language development concerns are observed, collaboration with SENCO and other specialists is advised for targeted support.

Pause for Reflection

In contemplating the critical influence of parents and carers in shaping a child's language growth, how do you currently engage with families to strengthen the link between home and school?

Implementing Targeted Vocabulary Interventions

The intervention can be structured within small groups or one-to-one, depending on each child's specific needs and the commonality of their vocabulary challenges. This flexible approach allows for a more personalised and effective method of support. Small group interventions can benefit children with similar vocabulary needs. Conversely, one-to-one sessions are ideal for addressing more unique or intensive vocabulary needs that require individual attention.

Ideally, these vocabulary interventions should be conducted daily to ensure consistency and to reinforce learning. The sessions should be led by either a teacher or a support staff member with a high proficiency level in language development. The consistent involvement of skilled educators is crucial for maintaining the quality and effectiveness of the intervention, providing the children with reliable guidance and support.

The structure of these interventions aligns with Rosenshine's Principles of Instruction and the GUIDE model, albeit with a focus on targeted language support. The effectiveness of vocabulary interventions hinges on their precise alignment with each child's specific needs. Here is where the role of the teacher becomes crucial, requiring astute assessment skills to identify and prioritise the most significant areas for development. Teachers must carefully evaluate each child's language attainment to determine what vocabulary needs to be taught and when, based on the individual gaps identified.

Depending on the nature of these gaps, the intervention strategies may vary. Sometimes, they might align closely with the vocabulary taught in the whole-class setting. In other cases, the interventions might need to be distinct from the classroom curriculum to meet the child's unique requirements. Additionally, there might be scenarios where a 'pre-teaching' approach is necessary; this involves providing those who need it with supplementary vocabulary lessons before introducing a new topic, ensuring they are equipped with the language required to engage with the upcoming content fully.

A critical aspect of these interventions is their temporal nature. Viewing them not as indefinite solutions but as temporary support mechanisms to enable children to access and keep pace with their peers is essential. The goal is for interventions to be a stepping stone towards independent learning, not a perpetual requirement. Each child's learning journey is different, and while some may need extended support, others will quickly bridge their gaps and no longer require additional interventions.

It is also essential to maintain high expectations for all children, regardless of their current level of need. In my experience, setting high expectations for children leads to remarkable outcomes, with children rising to meet these challenges accompanied by smiles on their faces. There is a profound power in believing in the potential of every child, regardless of their starting point or the obstacles they may face. This belief is not just a motivational tool; it shapes how we interact with and support our students.

When children sense that their teachers and caregivers have confidence in their abilities, it instils a sense of self-belief and determination. It encourages a positive learning attitude and a willingness to try, even when faced with challenging tasks.

As educators, our unwavering belief in every child's potential is a core component of their growth and success. This belief transforms learning challenges into opportunities for triumph and self-discovery. Interventions should not lead to pigeonholing children or limiting their potential for success. Instead, they should be seen as an empowering tool that helps each child reach their full potential. The overarching aim is to empower children with the skills and confidence they need to succeed, not just in the present but throughout their educational journey.

GUIDE Framework for Intervention

I will focus on the first three parts of the GUIDE framework as the final two elements remain the same, as discussed in other parts of the book.

Table 9.1 Suggestion Questions/Conversations to have When Building Relationships with Parents and Carers

Gather	• Focus the review on words that children find challenging to remember. • Tailor review to each child's specific difficulties in retention. • Begin sessions with flashcards displaying images/symbols and words. • The teacher pronounces the word first, followed by the child, to reinforce the correct pronunciation. • Adjust the pace of the review to suit the child. • Use the Language Treasure Box containing objects/images representing taught vocabulary. • During sessions, select items from the box to prompt identification and description by the child. • Encourage children to act out words or use them in context. • Play short, interactive vocabulary games. • Design games to be fun and dynamic, aiding in vocabulary retrieval.
Unveil	• Focus on one new word per session, possibly extending over 2–3 sessions for deeper understanding. • Aim for introducing 2–3 new words per week. • Use a Language Box to store objects and images representing new vocabulary. • When introducing a word, present a flashcard and a tangible object or photograph. • Place the item in the Language Box after the session for use in later reviews during the Gather portion of the next lesson. • Employ gestures, facial expressions and body language for teaching new words. • Model the use of the word in a variety of contexts. • Use 'My Turn, Your Turn' (you say, pupils repeat) so children can orally rehearse. • Connect new vocabulary words with pupils' prior experiences to create meaningful associations.
Interact	Facilitate oral practice of new vocabulary words. • Offer sentence frames or starters to scaffold pupils' verbal practice. • Use games and activities to engage pupils in active vocabulary practice. • Provide practical opportunities for children to use the vocabulary in context. • Continue to model words in sentence context and use lots of 'My Turn, Your Turn' exercises.

Gather

In the intervention process, reviewing previously learned vocabulary is especially crucial for children who find remembering challenging. This stage must be meticulously planned, keeping each child's specific difficulties in mind. For some, retaining new words can be a significant hurdle, making this stage a vital part of their learning. The review should focus intensively on words they find hard to remember. This targeted approach ensures that the review process is not just a repetition but a strategic reinforcement, helping to solidify the most difficult words for the child to retain.

As in whole-class teaching, begin using flashcards with images and symbols alongside each word. The teacher pronounces the word first and then the child repeats it, ensuring correct pronunciation and auditory reinforcement. Ensure that you work at the child's pace. You may need to do this a few times, which is acceptable. Following this, the child is encouraged to define the word. This process should be strongly supported by sentence structure assistance from the adult, tailored to the child's specific level of language development.

Alongside this, implement a 'Language Treasure Box'. This box should be filled with various objects and images, each representing different vocabulary words taught. After teaching a new word, place a related item or picture in the box; this will be discussed in more detail in the Unveil section below.

During each session, take items from the box, prompting children to identify and describe them, reinforcing their memory and understanding. Ask children to act out the word in some way – this is always lots of fun and gets the children on their feet and involved in the lesson.

Following this, engaging the children in brief vocabulary games effectively supports retrieval. Games should be fun and interactive, helping children recall and use the words they have learned in a dynamic setting. These games should be quick and lively.

Unveil

A careful and tailored approach is essential in adapting the 'Unveil' stage for vocabulary interventions. The focus should be on introducing new words in a way that is manageable, with only one word introduced. This word should be focused on where necessary across 2–3 sessions to ensure that it is understood. It is optional to introduce a new word every session; rather, aim for 2–3 words per week.

The use of a Language Box is a key element in this stage. The box should be used to place objects and images representing new vocabulary words. When introducing a new word during a vocabulary intervention session, use the flashcard that features both the word and its symbol. Alongside this, present a tangible object or photograph visually representing the word.

For instance, if the new word is 'cow', you could show a toy cow or a picture of a cow alongside the flashcard. At the end of the session, the item representing 'cow' is placed into the Language Box. The process helps consolidate the learning and prepares the object for use in the Gather phase of the subsequent lesson, aiding in review and reinforcement.

Non-verbal communication plays a crucial role in teaching new words, especially for children still developing their language skills or learning English as an additional language. Gestures, facial expressions and body language can be powerful tools to convey the meanings of words without relying solely on verbal explanations. For instance, when teaching the word 'jump', an educator can physically jump to demonstrate the action, making the concept clear and memorable.

The other elements of the GUIDE model, as discussed in Chapter 5, should also be used in this section of the intervention.

Interact

In the 'Interact' phase of the GUIDE model, the focus shifts to children using vocabulary within interactive activities and games, a crucial component of the intervention. Here, you provide children with practical opportunities to use the new vocabulary in enjoyable contexts. Through carefully selected games and activities, children can practise and reinforce their newly acquired words, enhancing both their understanding and ability to use them in conversation.

In this section, children may be interacting with each other or with whoever is facilitating the session, depending on whether they are working in a small group or one-to-one with the teacher. Below are some game examples, with further examples in Chapter 5.

Game Examples

Vocabulary Gallery – Give children a sheet with several large squares with space to draw. When the teacher announces a word, pupils illustrate it in their square. For adjectives, attach the word to a noun – e.g., big dog. A points system can be added, but it isn't necessary. This game can also be adapted for one-to-one sessions, where the child competes against the teacher, making it suitable for individual interventions.

Vocabulary Bean Bag Toss – Spread flashcards face down on the floor. Each card has the word's corresponding image or symbol that children associate with the word. Students toss a bean bag onto a card and then identify the word related to the image on the card they hit. If they correctly identify the word, they keep the card; if not, the card stays on the floor. For added challenge, children can earn bonus points by using the word in a sentence, with the teacher's support. The game ends when all the cards are collected and the student with the most cards is declared the winner.

Rhythmic Word Beats – Equip each child with a simple rhythm instrument. Display images of words with multiple syllables and pronounce them slowly. Children take turns to beat the rhythm of the syllables.

Study the Scene – Show a picture containing recent vocabulary words. It only needs to be a simple drawing made by the teacher on an easel incorporating recent vocabulary words; the emphasis is on the vocabulary the drawing represents. Ask the children to study it and describe what they can see in the picture using complete sentences.

Teach the Puppet – Introduce a puppet and tell the children that it is learning new words. Ask them to explain a word definition to the puppet, which then 'repeats' the definition back using the precise definition; children then repeat the precise definition.

Case Study

In his mixed Reception and Year 1 class, Mr T. embraces a proactive approach to supporting children who need additional help with vocabulary acquisition. His classroom is a hub of inclusivity and tailored support, catering to children who require additional support in vocabulary development alongside whole-class vocabulary teaching.

Mr T. begins by establishing strong connections with parents and carers, understanding each child's unique background and language exposure. This foundational work is critical in understanding where each child is on their learning journey.

Mr T. takes a comprehensive approach to preparing for his Reception class. Before the school year begins, he visits each child's family home. During these visits, he brings a specially designed questionnaire to understand each child's language exposure, interests and potential learning needs. Recognising the diversity in his class, Mr T. ensures that these questionnaires are available in the home language of each family, if necessary, to facilitate clear and effective communication. This preparation allows him to gather valuable insights directly from parents and carers, enabling him to best support each child's vocabulary development from day one.

Upon the children's entry into reception, Mr T. conducts a child-friendly baseline assessment in all areas of learning. Using the data gathered, he immediately plans for targeted vocabulary intervention for those needing it. He designs these interventions meticulously and entrusts their delivery to Mr Mills, a Higher-Level Teaching Assistant (HLTA). This strategic approach ensures that each child receives the necessary support from the beginning of their educational journey, setting a strong foundation for their continued language development.

When delivering the vocabulary interventions, Mr Mills adapts to each child's pace, ensuring that they understand and remember the vocabulary. During the Gather stage of the GUIDE model, Mr Mills utilises flashcards with images and symbols to review previously learned words. He also incorporates a Language Treasure Box, which contains objects and images representing the words taught. This box becomes a central tool in his class, reinforcing new vocabulary.

In the Unveil phase, Mr Mills introduces new words using the Language Box, pairing flashcards with tangible objects or photographs. This method helps the children connect the word to a concrete representation.

In the Interact stage of his vocabulary teaching, Mr Mills uses a variety of engaging games to reinforce the use of new words in context. These games are designed to be interactive and educational, encouraging active participation from all students.

Mr Mills uses gestures, facial expressions and body language to support children with non-verbal communication needs. He demonstrates actions and emotions associated with new words, making them more accessible and understandable for all children, including those developing their language skills or learning English as an additional language.

Overall, the approaches of Mr T. and Mr Mills are characterised by their adaptability, empathy and commitment to meeting the diverse needs of their students. They believe in the potential of each child and strive to create an environment where every student is empowered to succeed in their language development.

KEY TAKEAWAYS

- Vocabulary interventions should be adaptable, using small group or one-to-one settings to cater to individual needs. Daily sessions led by skilled educators are vital for reinforcing learning and addressing specific vocabulary challenges.
- These interventions align with Rosenshine's Principles of Instruction and the GUIDE model, focusing on targeted language support. Assessing each child's language needs is crucial to determine the most effective intervention strategies.
- View interventions as temporary support mechanisms to bridge gaps in vocabulary understanding. Maintain high expectations for all children, believing in every child's potential and facilitating their journey towards independent learning.
- Adapt the first three stages of the GUIDE model – Gather, Unveil, Interact – for targeted vocabulary interventions, ensuring that activities and games are carefully selected to practise and reinforce new vocabulary in engaging and practical ways.

Pause for Reflection

Consider the children in your class currently receiving vocabulary interventions. Reflect on the duration of these interventions. Are they temporary or have they become an ongoing process? How can you adjust your strategies to ensure that these interventions serve as bridges to independent learning rather than indefinite support mechanisms?

SUMMING UP

As we conclude this chapter, I hope that it has illuminated the critical role of educators in bridging the gaps in vocabulary for children who require additional support, emphasising not just the filling of these gaps, but also the empowerment of both staff and students. We have delved into practical tools to enhance vocabulary acquisition, ensuring that each child's unique learning path is nurtured in an environment where they can thrive.

Our focus on building strong relationships with parents and carers and the implementation of effective assessment methods form the foundation for these interventions. We have explored how the GUIDE model, amended for intervention, provides a structured yet flexible approach to support each child's language development. The careful planning of activities, attention to each child's pace and the incorporation of engaging methods like the Language Treasure Box ensure that learning is both impactful and enjoyable.

I hope this chapter has been a testament to the belief that with the proper support and environment, every child can succeed in their language journey. The insights shared here aim to equip educators with the knowledge and confidence to create a learning atmosphere that is not only inclusive but also celebrates the potential of every young learner.

> **Pause for Reflection**
>
> Reflect on your current practices supporting children with additional vocabulary needs. How do you incorporate the strategies and tools discussed in this chapter, such as parental/carer engagement and the strategies within the GUIDE model, into your daily teaching? How can you further enhance your approach to ensure each child's unique language journey is supported and celebrated in your classroom environment?

ACTION PLAN

Table 9.2 The GUIDE model for intervention: a teaching framework I have developed to explicitly teach vocabulary in Reception and Key Stage 1

Gather	• Focus the review on words that children find challenging to remember.
	• Tailor review to each child's specific difficulties in retention.
	• Begin sessions with flashcards displaying images/symbols and words.
	• The teacher pronounces the word first, followed by the child, to reinforce correct pronunciation.
	• Adjust the pace of the review to suit the child.
	• Use the Language Treasure Box containing objects/images representing taught vocabulary.
	• During sessions, select items from the box to prompt identification and description by the child.
	• Encourage children to act out words or use them in context.
	• Play short, interactive vocabulary games.
	• Design games to be fun and dynamic, aiding in vocabulary retrieval.

(Continued)

Table 9.2 The GUIDE model for intervention: a teaching framework I have developed to explicitly teach vocabulary in Reception and Key Stage 1 (*Continued*)

Unveil	• Focus on one new word per session, possibly extending over 2-3 sessions for deeper understanding. • Aim for introducing 2-3 new words per week. • Use a 'Language Box' to store objects and images representing new vocabulary. • When introducing a word, present a flashcard and a tangible object or photograph. • Place the item in the 'Language Box' after the session for use in later reviews during the GATHER portion of the next lesson. • Employ gestures, facial expressions, and body language for teaching new words. • Model the use of the word in a variety of contexts. • Use My Turn, Your Turn (You say, pupils repeat) so children can orally rehearse. • Connect new vocabulary words with pupils' prior experiences to create meaningful associations.
Interact	• Offer sentence frames or starters to scaffold pupils. • Use games and activities to engage pupils in active vocabulary practice. • Provide practical opportunities for children to use the vocabulary in context. • Continue to model words in sentence context and use lots of 'my turn, your turn.'

Table 9.3 Vocabulary Game Examples to be Used in the GUIDE Intervention/Interaction Phase

Game Examples
Vocabulary Gallery Give children a sheet with several large squares with space to draw. When the teacher announces a word, students illustrate it in their square. For adjectives, attach the word to a noun – e.g., 'big dog'. A points system can be added, but it isn't necessary. This game can also be adapted for one-to-one sessions, where the child competes against the teacher, making it suitable for individual interventions.
Vocabulary Bean Bag Toss Spread flashcards face down on the floor. Each card has the word's corresponding image or symbol that children associate with the word. Students toss a bean bag onto a card and then identify the word related to the image on the card they hit. If they correctly identify the word, they keep the card; if not, the card stays on the floor. For added challenge, children can earn bonus points by using the word in a sentence, with the teacher's support. The game ends when all cards are collected and the student with the most cards is declared the winner.
Rhythmic Word Beats Equip each child with a simple rhythm instrument. Display images of words with multiple syllables and pronounce them slowly. Children take turns beating the rhythm of the syllables.
Study the Scene Show a picture containing recent vocabulary words. It only needs to be a simple drawing made by the teacher on an easel incorporating recent vocabulary words; the emphasis is on the vocabulary the drawing represents. Ask the children to study it and describe what they can see in the picture using complete sentences.
Teach the Puppet Introduce a puppet and tell the children that it is learning new words. Ask them to explain a word definition to the puppet, which then 'repeats' the definition back using the precise definition; children then repeat the precise definition.

Table 9.4 An Action Plan for Practitioners to Assess their Current Practice and Consider their Next Steps in Order to Successfully Implement the Actions of Chapter 9

Action	Currently in Place	Next Steps
Before each new cohort, conduct home visits or one-to-one meetings to understand each child's home language environment and engagement. Use targeted questions to create a parent questionnaire to gain insights into the child's language exposure strengths.		
Review the baseline assessments to identify specific vocabulary gaps for each child and ascertain where interventions are needed. Decide whether interventions will be most effective in individual or small group settings.		
Plan and schedule regular intervention sessions, ensuring consistent and frequent practice.		
If necessary, provide training for support staff members who will be delivering the interventions. This training should cover the specific methods and materials to be used in the intervention. Work together with support staff to plan the intervention sessions, ensuring that they understand the objectives and strategies for each child.		
Conduct consistent (child-friendly) assessments to evaluate the child's understanding and use of new vocabulary.		

10 WHAT ARE MY NEXT STEPS?

It is crucial to recognise that the seeds of vocabulary that we plant in the fertile minds of young learners are not just words but tools for life. They empower children to navigate the world with confidence, articulate their thoughts and feelings, and engage with the human experience.

Every moment a child spends in our care is invaluable. As educators, we must recognise the weight of responsibility we hold. Each second, minute and hour that a child spends with us carries the potential to shape their future. This realisation calls for a purposeful approach to education, where every interaction, every lesson and every activity is thoughtfully designed to contribute positively to their development.

We are tasked with laying the foundation for lifelong learning. In doing so, we must also recognise the extraordinary power of language and vocabulary in our pupils' learning journey. Language is the key that unlocks numerous doors for children, opening up worlds of imagination, understanding and communication. It is through vocabulary that children learn to express themselves, to connect with others and to engage with the world around them.

A rich vocabulary can lay the groundwork for academic success and social interaction, enabling children to navigate the complexities of their environment and relationships. It equips them with the means to understand complex concepts, engage in deeper thinking and express themselves more effectively. In essence, investing in a child's vocabulary is investing in their future as confident, articulate and thoughtful individuals capable of navigating the diverse challenges of our world.

In this context, every word we teach, every conversation we have and every story we share is a stepping stone to a child's brighter future. The power of language is immense and as educators, we have the privilege and responsibility to harness this power for the betterment of our young learners.

Teaching, particularly in the Early Years, is a uniquely challenging and rewarding profession. It is often misunderstood, with outsiders casually referring to it as a time of 'just playing and painting'. However, those who have spent time in the Early Years know that it is immensely more complex and impactful. Being a Reception teacher is an extraordinary responsibility and privilege. We are laying the foundational building blocks of learning.

By understanding the pivotal role that vocabulary plays in a child's life, we can create more effective, supportive learning environments. For educators, this means integrating vocabulary instruction into your teaching. We have discussed the importance of blending explicit vocabulary instruction with play-based learning. The GUIDE framework reiterates the need for this balance, highlighting that one cannot exist effectively without the other. It is my hope that you will follow the steps laid out in this book and begin your vocabulary-teaching journey.

I encourage you to pause and consider how you will now approach vocabulary instruction. Reflect on how you will make vocabulary learning an integral part of your day.

Every word taught and every concept introduced shapes a child's understanding of the world. Vocabulary teaching, in this context, is a vital tool. As educators, we owe it to our children to provide them with the richest language environment possible. We are not just teaching words; we are opening doors to a world of understanding. It is why our role is so critical and why we must approach vocabulary teaching with the utmost dedication and care.

Words are powerful.

Pause for Reflection

As you embark on the journey of implementing the GUIDE framework in your teaching practice, what are the initial steps you plan to take? Reflect on how you will begin to integrate this framework into your daily routines and teaching strategies to enrich the vocabulary learning experience for your pupils. Consider the specific actions you will take to ensure that the principles of the GUIDE model become a seamless and effective part of your classroom environment.

REFERENCES

Baker, E.L., Croot, K., Clibbon, G., Ingram, J. and Webster, R. (2014) 'Supporting the development of children with special educational needs: A qualitative exploration of pre-school staff's perspectives', *Journal of Research in Special Educational Needs*, 14 (3): 170–8.

Beck, I.L., McKeown, M.G. and Kucan, L. (2002) *Bringing Words to Life: Robust Vocabulary Instruction*. New York: Guilford Press.

Beck, I.L., McKeown, M.G. and Kucan, L. (2013) *Bringing Words to Life: Robust Vocabulary Instruction*. New York: Guilford Press.

Brysbaert, M., Stevens, M., Mandera, P. and Keuleers, E. (2016) 'How many words do we know? Practical estimates of vocabulary size dependent on word definition, the degree of language input and the participant's age', *Frontiers in Psychology*, 7. Retrieved from: https://doi.org/10.3389/fpsyg.2016.01116

Carey, B., Bartlett, M., Deveau, J. and Rigoli, D. (2019) 'What makes a word hard to learn? Insights from developmental and experimental studies', *Topics in Cognitive Science*, 11 (3): 522–36.

Caviglioli, O. (2019) *Dual Coding With Teachers*. Melton, Woodbridge: John Catt Educational.

Cepeda, N. J., Vul, E., Rohrer, D., Wixted, J. T., and Pashler, H. (2008). Spacing effects in learning: A temporal ridgeline of optimal retention. *Psychological Science*, 19(11), 1095–1102.

Child Poverty Action Group (2023) 'Child poverty facts and figures'. Retrieved from: www.cpag.org.uk/child-poverty-facts-and-figures

Cunningham, A.E. and Stanovich, K.E. (1997) 'Early reading acquisition and its relation to reading experience and ability 10 years later'. *Developmental Psychology*, 33 (6): 934–45.

Department for Education (2017) 'Unlocking talent, fulfilling potential: A plan for improving social mobility through eduction'. Retrieved from: https://assets.publishing.service.gov.uk/media/5a82c6cb40f0b62305b94499/Social_Mobility_Action_Plan_-_for_printing.pdf

Department for Education (2021a) 'Changes to the Early Years Foundation Stage (EYFS) framework'. Retrieved from: www.gov.uk/government/publications/changes-to-the-early-years-foundation-stage-eyfs-framework/

Department for Education (2021b) 'Development Matters: Non-statutory curriculum guidance for the early years foundation stage'. Retrieved from: www.gov.uk/government/publications/development-matters–2

Department for Education (2021c) 'Statutory framework for the early years foundation stage: Setting the standards for learning, development and care for children from birth to five'. Retrieved from: https://assets.publishing.service.gov.uk/government/uploads/system/uploads/attachment_data/file/974907/EYFS_framework_-_March_2021.pdf

Department for Education (2021d) 'Statutory framework for the early years foundation stage: Setting the standards for learning, development and care for children from birth to five. Retrieved from https://assets.publishing.service.gov.uk/media/65aa5e42ed27ca001327b2c7/EYFS_statutory_framework_for_group_and_school_based_providers.pdf

Di Liberto, G.M., O'Sullivan, J., Lalor, E.C. and Dockrell, R. (2020) 'Nursery rhymes are optimal for helping infants detect and associate sounds with language', *Nature Communications*.

Di Liberto, G.M., Attaheri, A., Cantisani, G., Reilly, R.B., Choisdealbha, Á.N., Rocha, S. ... and Goswami, U. (2023) Emergence of the cortical encoding of phonetic features in the first year of life. *Nature Communications*, 14.

Dowling, M. (2018) 'Adapting teaching to accommodate learning styles: Accommodating and teaching to learning styles', *Journal of Education and Learning*, 7 (1): 112–22.

Duff, F.J. and Hulme, C. (2012) 'The role of children's phonological and semantic knowledge in learning to read words', *Scientific Studies of Reading*, 16 (6): 504–25.

Education Endowment Foundation (EEF) (2021) 'Oral language interventions'. Retrieved from: https://educationendowmentfoundation.org.uk/evidence-summaries/teaching-learning-toolkit/oral-language-interventions/

Fabriz, S., Mendzheritskaya, J. and Stehle, S. (2021) 'Impact of synchronous and asynchronous settings of online teaching and learning in higher education on students' learning experience during COVID-19', *Frontiers in Psychology*, 12. Retrieved from: https://doi.org/10.3389/fpsyg.2021.733554

Fernald, A., Marchman, V.A. and Weisleder, A. (2013) 'SES differences in language processing skill and vocabulary are evident at 18 months', *Developmental Science*, 16 (2): 234–48.

Fisher, K.R., Hirsh-Pasek, K., Golinkoff, R.M. and Gryfe, S.G. (2013) 'Conceptual split? Parents' and experts' perceptions of play in the 21st century', *Journal of Applied Developmental Psychology*, 34 (4): 173-80.

Geary, D.C. (2005) *The Origin of Mind: Evolution of Brain, Cognition, and General Intelligence*. American Psychological Association.

Golinkoff, R.M. and Hirsh-Pasek, K. (2006) 'The emergentist coalition model for language acquisition: Taking stock and moving forward'. In K. Hirsh-Pasek and R.M. Golinkoff (eds), *Action Meets Word: How Children Learn Verbs*. Oxford: Oxford University Press. pp. 367–95.

Gough, P.B. and Tunmer, W.E. (1986) 'Decoding, reading, and reading disability. RASE: *Remedial and Special Education*, 7 (1): 6–10

Hamre, B. and Pianta, R. (2001) 'Early teacher–child relationships and the trajectory of children's school outcomes through eighth grade', *Child Development*, 72 (2): 625–38.

Hart, B. and Risley, T.R. (1995) *Meaningful Differences in the Everyday Experience of Young American Children*. Baltimore, MD: Brookes.

REFERENCES

Hart, B. and Risley, T.R. (2003) 'The early catastrophe: The 30 million word gap by age 3', *American Educator*, 27 (1): 4–9.

Hirsch, E.D., Jr (2003) 'Reading comprehension requires knowledge—of words and the world', *American Educator*, 27 (1): 10–13, 16–22, 28–9, 48.

Hirsh-Pasek, K., Adamson, L.B., Bakeman, R., Owen, M.T., Golinkoff, R.M., Pace, A., … and Suma, K. (2015) 'The contribution of early communication quality to low-income children's language success', *Psychological Science*, 26 (7): 1071–83.

Hopman, E.W.M. and MacDonald, M.C. (2018) Production Practice During Language Learning Improves Comprehension. *Psychological Science, 29*(6), 961–971. Retrieved from: https://doi.org/10.1177/0956797618754486.

Hughes, C. (2009) 'Ensuring quality early childhood education and care', *OECD Education Working Papers, No. 24*. Paris: OECD Publishing.

Jackendoff, R. (2012) *A User's Guide to Thought and Meaning*. Oxford: Oxford University Press.

Jones, K. (2019) *Retrieval Practice: Research & Resources for Every Classroom: Resources and Research for Every Classroom*. Melton: John Catt Educational.

Kirschner, P.A., Sweller, J. and Clark, R.E. (2006) 'Why minimal guidance during instruction does not work: An analysis of the failure of constructivist, discovery, problem-based, experiential, and inquiry-based teaching', *Educational Psychologist*, 41 (2): 75–86.

Kirschner, P.A. and Hendrick, C. (2020) *How Learning Happens: Seminal Works in Educational Psychology and What They Mean in Practice*. Abingdon: Routledge.

McKague, M., Pratt, C. and Johnston, M.B. (2001) 'The effect of oral vocabulary on reading visually novel words: A comparison of the dual-route-cascaded and triangle frameworks', *Cognition*, 80 (3): 231–62.

Montag, J.L., Jones, M.N. and Smith, L.B. (2018) 'Quantity and diversity: Simulating early word learning environments', *Cognitive Science*, 42 (2): 375–412.

Nagy, W.E. and Herman, P.A. (1987) 'Breadth and depth of vocabulary knowledge: Implications for acquisition and instruction'. In M.G. McKeown and M.E. Curtis (eds), *The Nature of Vocabulary Acquisition*. Mahwah, NJ: Lawrence Erlbaum Associates. (pp. 19–35).

Nation, I.S.P. (2001) *Learning Vocabulary in Another Language*. Cambridge: Cambridge University Press.

National Early Literacy Panel (2008) 'Developing early literacy: Report of the National Early Literacy Panel'. Rockville, MD.

National Literacy Trust (2017) '1 in 8 disadvantaged children in the North East don't own a single book'. Retrieved from: https://literacytrust.org.uk/news/1-8-disadvantaged-children-uk-dont-own-single-book/

National Reading Technical Assistance Center (2010) 'Research-based practices for effective vocabulary instruction'. Rockville, MD.

New South Wales Department of Education (2023) 'Explicit teaching'. Retrieved from: https://education.nsw.gov.au/about-us/education-data-and-research/what-works-best/teachers/theme-explicit-teaching

Pearson, H.C. and Wilbiks, J.M.P. (2021) 'Effects of audiovisual memory cues on working memory recall', *Vision (Basel)*, 5 (1): 14.

REFERENCES

Pellegrini, A.D. and Galda, L. (1993) 'Ten years after: A reexamination of symbolic play and literacy research', *Reading Research Quarterly*, 28 (2): 163–75.

Rosenshine, B. (2012) 'Principles of instruction: Research-based strategies that all teachers should know', *American Educator*, 36 (1): 12–19.

Sammons, P., Elliot, K., Sylva, K., Melhuish, E. Siraj-Blatchford, I. and Taggart, B. (2004) 'The impact of pre-school on young children's cognitive attainments at entry to Reception', *British Educational Research Journal*, 30 (5): 691–712.

Soderman, T., Bjork, R.A. and Bjork, E.L. (2008) 'Improving students' long-term knowledge retention through personalized review', *Psychological Science*, 19 (3): 209–15.

Speech and Language UK (n.d.) 'Scale of the issue'. Retrieved from: https://speechandlanguage.org.uk/talking-point/for-professionals/information-for-inspectors/scale-of-the-issue/

Sperry, D.E., Sperry, L.L. and Miller, P.J. (2019) 'Reexamining the verbal environments of children from different socioeconomic backgrounds', *Child Development*, 90 (4): 1303–18.

Stahl, S.A. and Nagy, W.E. (2005) *Teaching Word Meanings*. Mahwah, NJ: Lawrence Erlbaum Associates.

Sweller, J. (1988) 'Cognitive load during problem-solving: Effects on learning', *Cognitive Science*, 12 (2): 257–85.

Toub, T.S., Hassinger-Das, B., Ilgaz, H., Weisberg, D.S., Hirsh-Pasek, K. and Golinkoff, R.M. (2018) 'The language of play: Developing preschool vocabulary through play following shared book-reading', *Early Childhood Research Quarterly*, 45: 1–17.

Van Merriënboer, J.J. and Sweller, J. (2005) 'Cognitive load theory and complex learning: Recent developments and future directions', *Educational Psychology Review*, 17 (2): 147–77.

Vygotsky, L. S. (1978). *Mind in Society: The Development of Higher Psychological Processes*. Harvard University Press.

Wasik, B.A. and Bond, M.A. (2001) 'Beyond the pages of a book: Interactive book reading and language development in preschool classrooms', *Journal of Educational Psychology*, 93 (2): 243–50.

Weinstein, Y. and Sumeracki, M. (2018) *Understanding How We Learn: A Visual Guide*. Abingdon: Routledge.

Weisleder, A. and Fernald, A. (2013) 'Talking to children matters: Early language experience strengthens processing and builds vocabulary', *Psychological Science*, 24 (11): 2143–52.

Whitebread, D., Coltman, P., Jameson, H. and Lander, R. (2012) 'Play, cognition and self-regulation: What exactly are children learning when they learn through play?' *Educational and Child Psychology*, 29 (1): 40–52.

Zadina, J.N. (2014) *Multiple Pathways to the Student Brain*. San Francisco, CA: Jossey-Bass.

Zosh, J.M., Fisher, K., Golinkoff, R.M. and Hirsh-Pasek, K. (2018) 'The ultimate block party: Bridging the science of learning and the importance of play', *Child Development*, 89 (4): E488–E492.

INDEX

Page numbers in **bold** refer to tables.

active engagement, 23
active learning, **30**, 31
adult–child interactions, 25
Areas of Learning, 21–26, **22**
assessment, 136–138

Baker, E.L., 20
Beck, I.L., 47, 49, **49**
bilingualism, 111. *See also* English as an Additional Language (EAL)
biologically primary knowledge, 33, 35–37
biologically secondary knowledge, 33, 35–37
Bond, M.A., 9

carers. *See* parents and carers
Carey, B., 20
Carle, E., 85
Characteristics of Effective Learning (CoEL), 29–31, **30**
charades, 74
child-centred approach, 10, 16, 30–32, 41
Choose the Right One (game), 74
class culture, 10–11
Cognitive Load Theory (CLT), 33–34, 41–44, 49, 63, 68
Communication and Language (Area of Learning), 21–26, **22**
concept stories, 91–93
concept words
　overview of, 81–83
　Interact stage of GUIDE model and, 89–96
　Unveil stage of GUIDE model and, 83–89, **85**, 95–96
confidence, 24–25
conversational observation, 108
costumes, 126–127
creative and critical thinking, **30**, 31

Department for Education (DfE), 8, 16, 31. *See also* Development Matters; Early Years Foundation Stage (EYFS)
Development Matters, 15, 16–17, 29–31, **30**

Di Liberto, G.M., 108–109
direct instruction. *See* explicit teaching and direct instruction
dress-up costumes, 126–127
Dual Coding Theory, 68, 86–87

Early Learning Goals (ELGs), 26–29, **27–28**, 100–101, **101**
Early Years Foundation Stage (EYFS)
　overview of, 15–17
　action plan for practitioners, **32**
　Areas of Learning in, 21–26, **22**
　Development Matters and, 15, 16–17, 29–31, **30**
　direct teaching and, 15–16, 17, 19, 22–25, 30–32
　Early Learning Goals (ELGs) and, 26–29, **27–28**
　essential principles of, 17–21
　oral language and, 100
Education Endowment Foundation (EEF), 100
effective learning, 29–31, **30**
eleven-plus system, 34
enabling environments, 9, 19–20
English as an Additional Language (EAL)
　assessment and, 136
　Demonstrate stage of GUIDE model and, 104
　families and, 111–112
　pre-teaching and, 20
　support for, 18
　Unveil stage of GUIDE model and, 68, 140–141
　See also inclusive education
etymology, 6
explicit teaching and direct instruction
　Cognitive Load Theory (CLT) and, 63
　Early Years Foundation Stage (EYFS) and, 15–16, 17, 19, 22–25, 30–32
　GUIDE model and, 13, 63–64, **64**, 91, 95
　oracy skills and, 131
　play-based learning and, 9, 30–31, 36, 117–120, 128, 149–150

role and importance of, 11–12
Rosenshine's Principles of Instruction and, 38–41, 63
vocabulary levels and, **49–50**, 51–53
Expressive Arts and Design (Area of Learning), 21–22, **22**

families. *See* parents and carers
Fernald, A., 2, 36
fluency, 24–25

games and activities, 73–75, 90–91, 93–95, 142–143, 145. *See also* play and play-based learning
Geary, D.C., 33, 35–37
Gough, P.B., 7
grammar, 4
grammar schools, 34
graphemes, 5, 38–39, 105
group activities monitoring, 108
GUIDE model
  overview of, 13–14, 64, **64**
  Demonstrate stage of, **64**, 100–107, **102**, 114
  Embed stage of, **64**, 100–102, **102**, 107–114, **114–115**
  Gather stage of, **64**, 65–67, 77–78, **79**, 140–141, **140**
  inclusive education and, 139–145, **140**, **145–146**
  Interact stage of, 64, 72–78, 89–96, **140**, 142–144
  Rosenshine's Principles of Instruction and, 40
  Unveil stage of, **64**, 67–72, 77–78, 83–89, **85**, 95–96, **140**, 141–142
  vocabulary levels and, 50, 52
guided play, 118

Hamre, B., 18
Hart, B., 2
Hendrick, C., 86–87
high-quality conversations, 23
Hirsch, E.D., Jr, 7
Hirsh-Pasek, K., 36
home visits, 134–135
Hopman, E.W.M., 72

inclusive education
  action plan for practitioners, **145–146**
  assessment and, 136–138
  direct teaching and, 131
  Early Years Foundation Stage (EYFS) and, 20
  empowering language in, 132–133, 144–145
  GUIDE model and, 104, 139–145, **140**, **145–146**
  role of parents and carers in, 134–136, 145
  Rosenshine's Principles of Instruction and, 131–132, 138–139
  targeted vocabulary interventions and, 138–139
  See also English as an Additional Language (EAL)

Jackendoff, R., 4
Jeffers, O., 85

Kirschner, P.A., 86–87
Kucan, L., 47

language comprehension, 24–25
Language Treasure Box, 141, 145
Literacy (Area of Learning), 21–22, **22**, 24–25
long-term memory
  Cognitive Load Theory (CLT) and, 42
  Early Years Foundation Stage (EYFS) and, 19–20, 24
  GUIDE model and, 65–66
  retrieval practice and, 12
  Rosenshine's Principles of Instruction and, 42, 65
  vocabulary levels and, 51

MacDonald, M.C., 72
Makaton, 87–88
Mathematics (Area of Learning), 21–22, **22**
McKeown, M.G., 47
meaning, 4–7
memory
  Cognitive Load Theory (CLT) and, 41–42
  Early Years Foundation Stage (EYFS) and, 19–20, 24
  GUIDE model and, 65–66
  inclusive education and, 141
  retrieval practice and, 12
  Rosenshine's Principles of Instruction and, 42, 65
  visual aids and, 105
  vocabulary levels and, 51
modelling, 23, 102–104
Montag, J.L., 3
morphemes, 5
My Turn, Your Turn strategy, 69–70, 87
Mystery Bag (game), 75

National Early Literacy Panel (NELP), 72
National Literacy Trust, 10
National Reading Technical Assistance Center, 72

INDEX

New South Wales Department of Education, 119
nursery rhymes, 108–109

oral language and vocabulary
    Demonstrate stage of GUIDE model and, 100–107, 114
    direct teaching and, 131
    Embed stage of GUIDE model and, 100–102, 107–114, **114–115**
    Interact stage of GUIDE model and, 72, 90
    role and importance of, 7, 99–100, **101**

Pair and Share (activity), 90
parents and carers
    Early Years Foundation Stage (EYFS) and, 18–20
    Embed stage of GUIDE model and, 110–113, **115**
    inclusive education and, 134–136, 145
    play-based learning and, 124–125, **129**
peer practice, 72–73
Personal, Social and Emotional Development (Area of Learning), 21–22, **22**, 25
phonemes, 4, 38–39, 105
phonics, 3–4, 119
phonology, 69–70, 88
Physical Development (Area of Learning), 21–22, **22**
Pianta, R., 18
Pictionary (game), 74
play and play-based learning
    action plan for practitioners, **129**
    Development Matters and, 30, **30**
    direct teaching and, 9, 30–31, 36, 117–120, 128, 149–150
    Embed stage of GUIDE model and, 108
    Geary's framework and, 35, 36–37
    role and importance of, 12–13, 117–118, 128
    Rosenshine's Principles of Instruction and, 39–41
    taught vocabulary and, 120–123
    vocabulary-rich play environments and, 123–127
    See also games and activities
play scripts, 123–126
polysemy, 6
positive relationships, 18–19
poverty, 2
pre-teaching, 20, 139
props, 126–127

recognition systems, 104
register, 6
retrieval practice, 12
reward systems, 104
Rhythmic Word Beats, 142
Risley, T.R., 2
role-play, 24, 30
Rosenshine's Principles of Instruction
    overview of, 33–34, 37–41, **37**, 42–44, **45**
    direct teaching and, 38–41, 63
    GUIDE model and, 65
    inclusive education and, 131–132, 138–139

Sammons, P., 19
semantics, 6
sentence frames, 72
short-term memory, 12
signing systems, 87–88
socioeconomic factors, 2, 8
Soderman, T., 65
songs, 108–109, **114–115**
spaced retrieval practice, 65
Special Educational Needs (SEN), 20, 88. *See also* inclusive education
speech, language and communication needs (SLCN), 8
Sperry, D.E., 2
storybook words, 56–59
storytelling, 24, 91–93
Storytelling Circle (game), 74
storytime, 3, 56–59, 103, 106, 108
Study the Scene (game), 142–143
Sumeracki, M., 65
symbols. *See* visual aids and symbols
syntax, 5

Teach the Puppet (game), 143
topic words, 53–56, **55**
Tunmer, W.E., 7

Understanding the World (Area of Learning), 21–22, **22**, 25
unique child, 16, 17–18

visual aids and symbols
    Demonstrate stage of GUIDE model and, 105–106
    Gather stage of GUIDE model and, 65, 74, 140
    inclusive education and, 140, 141
    Unveil stage of GUIDE model and, 68, 77, 86–88, 92, 96, 141
Vocabulary Bean Bag Toss, 142
vocabulary charts, 105–106
vocabulary enrichment, 23
Vocabulary Gallery, 142

INDEX

vocabulary levels, 49–53, **49–50**
vocabulary-rich play environments, 123–127
vocabulary teaching, 10–13, **14**. *See also* GUIDE model; words

Wasik, B.A., 9
Weinstein, Y., 65
Weisleder, A., 36
Whitebread, D., 30
whole-class teaching, 9, 133
Word Bingo (game), 74
word classes, 5
Word Detective (game), 74
Word of the Day, 66
Word Relay (game), 66
word selection
    overview of, 47–48
    action plan for practitioners, **61**

concept words and, 83–86, **85**
role of teachers and, 59–60
storybook words and, 56–59
topic words and, 53–56, **55**
vocabulary levels and, 49–53, **49–50**
Word Thoughts (game), 75
Word Wall Ball (game), 74
word walls, 105–106
Word Wizard charts, 104
words
    breadth and depth of vocabulary and, 7
    Early Years gap and, 8–9
    meaning and, 4–7
    role and importance of, 1–3, 149–150
    See also GUIDE model
working memory, 41–42

Zosh, J.M., 118